# ROOMING IN THE MASTER'S HOUSE

# ROOMING IN THE MASTER'S HOUSE

## POWER AND PRIVILEGE IN THE RISE OF BLACK CONSERVATISM

## MOLEFI K. ASANTE and RONALD E. HALL

PARADIGM PUBLISHERS

*Boulder & London*

Copyright © 2011 Paradigm Publishers

Published in the United States by Paradigm Publishers, 2845 Wilderness Place, Suite 200, Boulder, CO 80301 USA.

Paradigm Publishers is the trade name of Birkenkamp & Company, LLC, Dean Birkenkamp, President and Publisher.

Library of Congress Cataloging-in-Publication Data

Asante, Molefi K., 1942–
　Rooming in the master's house : Power and Privilege in the Rise of Black Conservatism / Molefi K. Asante, Ronald E. Hall.
　　p. cm.
　Includes bibliographical references and index.
　ISBN 978-1-59451-890-4 (hardcover : alk. paper) — ISBN 978-1-59451-891-1 (pbk. : alk. paper)
　1. African Americans—Politics and government. 2. Conservatism—United States. 3. Slavery—United States—History. 4. African Americans—History. 5. African Americans—Social conditions. 6. African Americans—Intellectual life. 7. United States—Race relations—Political aspects. 8. United States—Politics and government. I. Hall, Ronald E. II. Title.
　E185.A82 2010
　323.1196'073—dc22

2010015512

Printed and bound in the United States of America on acid-free paper that meets the standards of the American National Standard for Permanence of Paper for Printed Library Materials.

Designed and Typeset by Straight Creek Bookmakers.

15  14  13  12  11    1  2  3  4  5

# Contents

Preface     *vii*

Chapter One
*Slave Psychology: The Shape of Race Relations*     1

Chapter Two
*Field Negroes and House Negroes*     25

Chapter Three
*House Negroes and the Crisis of Identity*     49

Chapter Four
*The Conservative Political Agenda*     79

Chapter Five
*Self-Mutilation in the Master's House*     107

Chapter Six
*Extending the Metaphors: Conservatives and Liberals*     135

References     *155*

Index     *163*

About the Authors     *167*

# *Preface*

Since the 2008 election of President Barack Obama, there has been a great rush to explain the nature of the African American political community. However, in the years leading up to his election by a progressive coalition of Americans supporting an agenda of change, black conservatives asserted one of the principal narratives opposing Obama's presidency: fear of his idea of black entitlements. Black conservatives represent a vocal minority within the Republican Party, although all black Republicans are not conservatives. Issues like rugged individualism, states' rights, American military supremacy, anti-abortion, gun rights, and unfettered capitalism have galvanized the dyed-in-the-wool black conservatives. For all practical purposes, these blacks are in the same tradition as conservative whites in the United States who have advanced the idea of the individual over the common good, American national exceptionalism among states, and unregulated capitalism. Michael Steele, for example, was elected the first black to chair the Republican National Committee right after the nation had chosen Obama as president, but he proclaimed the same exceptionalism as the white conservatives and made almost no outreach to the masses of African Americans. Furthermore, Steele, who has had a fiery, controversial, and agitative tenure since becoming the leader of the Republican National Committee in January 2009, also served as Lieutenant Governor of Maryland—the first African American elected to statewide office in the state—and chairman of the GOPAC, the Republicans' training and fundraising group. But it was as a commentator for Fox News that Steele showed his marbles, so to speak, to the Republicans as one who could "out-Republican" the most dyed-in-the-wool white conservative. Like Steele, most black conservatives share most of the attitudes of the white conservatives. Black conservatives have often articulated a nationalism that borders on jingoism and claimed special knowledge about the causes of poverty, inadequate health care, and poor education in some black communities. As such, they are the authentic sustainers of the status quo, however unequal, imprecise, and anti-African that status quo happens to be. Malcolm X had a term for them: house Negroes.

The term *house Negro* had its source in the separation of Africans from one another in an effort to maintain a duality in the plantation system of work and responsibility between the enslaved who worked in the fields and shops and those who were trusted enough to work in the master's house. During the enslavement, those Africans who were chosen to work in the big house, close to the white family, in time may have also been distinguished from those who worked in the fields by the lightness of their skin color. From the beginning of the African enslavement in America, white slave traders and slaveholders had complete access to enslaved females, who then produced children who struggled with their identities. They could easily see that in a mass of black faces, theirs was not nearly as black and indicated the presence of white paternity. This was an observable fact among the enslaved, as portrayed in Haile Gerima's famous film, *Sankofa,* but as we shall see, there were blacks produced from these liaisons for whom their status as descendants of rapists motivated them to fight slavery, oppose discrimination, and rebel against the prevailing social and political structure. Alas, however, most descendants of black women and white slaveholders did not follow this route during the early days of the enslavement. They were co-opted, so to speak, by the blandishments of racial hierarchy that promised them a "better" enslavement if they served the interests of the masters—who were often their fathers. They became good converts to the mentality of other house Negroes. Thus, separation from the masses was the key ingredient in the mixed messages of slavery and identity for the house Negro. By being separated from the masses, or the field Negroes, the house Negro developed a sense of being "special," "acceptable," and "different" from the collective masses of his own people; indeed, he was often embarrassed by the behavior, thinking, and beliefs of the field Negroes. The house Negro's relationship with the black collective weakened to the degree that he adopted the submissive and aggrandizing behaviors that made him useful to the white slave masters.

Thus, the house Negro was socialized in a different way than other blacks. He was often given trinkets, such as glass jars and pieces of silk, to memorialize the difference between himself and his community. At certain points, the house Negro became identified in the minds of other blacks with what could happen to blacks mentally when they submitted to the perils of human bondage and embraced the political and psychological directives of the dominant white power structure. Those directives, policies, rules, and privileges became, for the house Negro, manifested as white superiority. To him, they made it clear that everything the white slave owner did should be considered good, worthy of emulation, and legitimate. What the African did, on the contrary, should be seen as bad, incorrect, and derivative. The house Negro, then, believed in white supremacy almost as much as the white man believed in it. The social and political structure of slavery contrived this belief in white superiority in order to justify the European Slave Trade and the ensuing subjugation of Africans who reached the Americas bound in chains. However, these justifications were not enough to prevent the house Negro from believing in the ultimate power of white supremacy. Yet neither brutality nor bondage prevented house Negroes from casting their lots with whites; in most cases, no amount of hostility from the white plantation owners changed house Negroes' affection for their position with the white masters. Sometimes the house Negro's arguments were as anti-African as those of the white slave owner. The house Negro was an apologist for every cruel deed inflicted against progressive, self-respecting, and rebellious Africans. When Africans sought to escape from the plantation, they had to ensure that their plans would not get to the ears of the house Negro because, on more than one occasion, the house Negro was the instrument of death. Seeking methods to frustrate the interest of black people and serve the interest of the white slave master, to insinuate themselves into what they considered to be the good graces of the white master, became the constant task of the house Negro. The house Negroes named their children after the master. If the master's daughter were named Madison, Kennedy, Taylor, Ryan, or Wilson, then the house Negro would give his daughter the same name. He would ridicule the field Negroes for choosing "jungle" names when they gave their children African or African-derived names like Kiamuya, Eka, Tobolayefa, Tamieka, Shanika, Tamu, Fatou, Ama, Ayaana, or Akua. In contemporary times, the black conservatives often refer to African names as "ghetto" when a person expresses pride in her or his African culture and heritage. The house Negro might say, "Anyone can tell when she hears that name that the person is black," in the same way that one knows that a name such as Ogawa, Morikawa, Miike, or Suzuko is that of someone who is Japanese. What is wrong with people knowing that your name reflects your history and culture? Of course, nothing is wrong with this except that the house Negro sees these African names as being disloyal to the white slave master.

Furthermore, any opportunity to dispute an aggressive black person or to rebuke enslaved Africans planning to disrupt the plantation became a chance for the house Negro to demonstrate his love for the master. Of course, these were always unequal and unholy alliances because the white slave master often despised the house Negro more than he hated the field Negro. The house Negro was weak, could not be trusted, and would give incriminating information about his own children if he felt that they were trying to escape slavery. Thus, the house Negro is the figure for the contemporary black conservative, the house Negro's political descendant who has inherited the same spirit of cooperation with anti-African elements for his or her own self-interest. Black conservatives despise those who fight for liberation of the mind and the body. They resent the dignified struggle against injustice, seeing it as yet another attempt on the part of the black masses, the descendants of the field Negroes, to seek collective remedies. They are the anti-African Africans, the racists against themselves as Africans, the self-described individuals whose only ambition is self-centeredness as a means to distinguish themselves from the masses. They often despise themselves and, in despising themselves, find every opportunity to disown blackness, that is, African culture in any form: language, style, food, music, or philosophy. They are the white reactionaries' first line of attack against African Americans fighting for racial equality. They are the people who would sell their own mothers back into slavery if doing so would benefit them for a little while.

In 1963 Malcolm X gave a spirited account of the differences within the African American community regarding Civil and Human Rights. Malcolm X recalled that there were *house Negroes* and *field Negroes* with different orientations during the enslavement. Where you worked and how you worked impacted your consciousness. Like the Marxian analysis of the worker and the bourgeoisie, our analysis of the black political condition suggests that at times consciousness is often a matter of a person's place and type of work. The house Negro was sure to possess a different outlook on life than the field Negro who had never even passed the threshold of the master's big house. In the antebellum South, where slavery was the foundation of society, life for field Negroes amounted to little more than attempts to survive within a racist system of institutionalized oppression. Marked by skin color and condition of enslavement, being African was—for both field Negroes and house Negroes—a constant reminder of assigned inferiority invented for the political and social justification of the European Slave Trade. Thus, the history of bondage in the United States, with house Negroes assuming a role of support for the house whereas field Negroes were assigned to hard labor, loomed large, despite the fact that the founding documents that established the democratic union of the American states proclaimed lofty ideals of freedom and equality of all people.

Whites made distinctions between the enslaved Africans as a means of controlling large groups of people. Not all enslaved could work in the big house, and once the whites had secured their house Negroes, they also began the process of brainwashing them to be the servile, imitating, and obsequious humans the whites needed in order to control the majority of Africans on the plantation. Notwithstanding accusations of inferiority, life for the house Negro was never as bitter or brutal as that for the masses. Whites preferred the house Negroes and would depend on them to carry out the master's commands when the master was absent. They were chosen because they worked assiduously to separate themselves from other Africans. They would demonstrate to the white slave master that they did not like Africans any more than the white slave master. In fact, some would even claim that they were not Africans, despite the obvious African nature of their behavior, skin color, and condition of servitude.

Unlike the field Negroes who usually toiled from dawn to dusk under the relentless rays of unforgiving heat to produce the master's crop, the house Negro lived in relative ease in terms of physical toil. Furthermore, he ate scraps from the master's table, lived in a shack close to the master's house or under the master's roof, and otherwise did the master's bidding as told. When crops failed, the house Negro felt the master's pain. When field Negroes refused to work, the house Negroes would also bear the master's loss. In every way, the house Negroes identified with the master's family as a means to buffer themselves from the life of lowly field Negroes. The house Negro's greatest fear was the possibility that if he did not serve the master well, he could be removed from the house and sent to work in the field. Falling from the master's grace was a peril too unthinkable for the house Negro, who would therefore do anything to maintain favor, even report his own mother's attempt to escape.

Rooming in the master's house, these house Negroes took on many of the same attitudes about Africans as the masters. If the master of the house spoke disparagingly of Africans as "niggers," the house Negro used the same language when referring to other blacks. His actions were an iconography of self-hatred.

The American nation was born with several inherent contradictions. Famed white luminaries such as Thomas Jefferson and other signers of the Declaration of Independence in 1776 could not rescue such a profound political document from such moral transgressions as their support for slavery. Thus, the liberty of the whites and the enslavement of the Africans produced a mockery of justice. Even as whites ruled a nation won from oppression by the British and were able to promise freedom for Europeans who sought prosperity and equal opportunity, they also held in bondage millions of Africans. The obscenity of this duality was never lost in the thinking of enslaved Africans. In fact, the starkness of this contradiction was never so meaningful as when Frederick Douglass declared in his 1841 speech before a group of Americans in Rochester:

> What, to the American slave, is your Fourth of July? I answer: a day that reveals to him, more than all other days in the year, the gross injustice and cruelty to which he is the constant victim. To him, your celebration is a sham; your boasted liberty, an unholy license; your national greatness, swelling vanity; your sounds of rejoicing are empty and heartless; your denunciation of tyrants, brass-fronted impudence; your shouts of liberty and equality, hollow mockery; your prayers and hymns, your sermons and thanksgivings, with all your religious parade and solemnity, are, to Him, mere bombast, fraud, deception, impiety, and hypocrisy—a thin veil to cover up crimes which would disgrace a nation of savages. There is not a nation of savages. There is not a nation on the earth guilty of practices more shocking and bloody than are the people of the United States at this very hour. (Smith, 1969, p. 149)

Despite the rhetoric of individual liberty found in the speeches and writings of the early American leaders, the oppression of Africans remained an ever-present stain on the fabric of the democratic experiment. We believe that the legacy of the slave system is apparent in the daily struggles of African Americans today as they toil to overcome the yoke of institutionalized oppression, segregation, and racial discrimination as represented in lack of self-love, hatred of Africa, ignorance of culture and history, psychological dislocation, and post-traumatic stress syndrome. It is likewise apparent in the accusations from the late twentieth-century eugenicists, such as Richard Herrnstein and Charles Murray, who stoked the doctrine of white supremacy with their charges of black physical and mental inferiority (Herrnstein and Murray, 1996). Their arguments can be seen as enhancements of biological determinism. Using social aspects of biology, they repeat the constituents of Social Darwinism to demonstrate that there is a biological foundation to all human differences. Of course, this is a vast modification from the idea that Social Darwinism meant during the early twentieth century, the idea that all social reform was futile. Stephen Jay Gould, writing in the *New Yorker,* argued that

> The theory arose from a paradox of egalitarianism: as long as people remain on top of the social heap by accident of a noble name or parental wealth, and as long as members of despised castes cannot rise no matter what their talents, social stratification will not reflect intellectual merit, and brilliance will be distributed across all classes; but when true equality of opportunity is attained smart people rise and the lower classes become rigid, retaining only the intellectually incompetent. (Gould, 1994, November 28, p. 139)

Herrnstein and Murray, however, suggested there was an innate cognitive stratification, and the smoking gun for this claim was the differences in IQ scores among races, showing Asian superiority over Caucasians and the large difference between Caucasians over Africans. We have all heard this argument in one fashion or another because it coexists with the doctrine of white racial superiority. Even though it is fallacious, it remains a popular argument for those who believe in what it upholds. This is the arena of Arthur Jensen, William Shockley, and others who have spent time advocating white dominance based on heritability. However, the logic falters because the argument uses the substantial heritability within a group as an explanation of average differences among multiple groups. In other words, you can take a heritable trait, such as height, body shape, or weight—something not politically controversial—and measure all the females in a small, poverty-stricken South American village and discover that the average height is five feet four, but among tall mothers the average goes up to five feet six. Heritability within the village is high when the tall mothers five feet seven inches on average tend to have tall daughters and short mothers tend to have short daughters. This heritability might change if more food and better nutrition were introduced, and within a few generations the average height may be five feet eight for everyone. In the same way, the 12- to 15-point difference between whites and blacks will probably be wiped out when the socioeconomic conditions of the black community change. Of course, Herrnstein and Murray's work was interpreted as negative toward Africans. They tried to use moral justification for the physical and cultural exploitation of African masses. As in the past, the doctrine of white supremacy justified not just oppression but also discrimination such that the sons and daughters of former enslaved Africans remained locked in second-class citizenship long after the Civil War ended.

Yet it is clear in the first part of the twenty-first century that we are not out of the dense woods of racism. Even as we celebrated the 2008 election of Barack Obama as president of the United States, we were reminded of the issues that remain to be resolved in our democracy. Although the weight of chains no longer restricts us physically, they still restrict psychologically some among the sons and daughters of former enslaved Africans.

In this book, we are concerned with those Africans who, as the ideological descendants of house Negroes, find every achievement of African Americans problematic and who, because of their dedication to white supremacy, have become, by virtue of their commitment to a dead ideology, albatrosses around the necks of whites who once needed them. By their own accord, the spiritual descendants of house Negroes distance themselves from modern-day field Negroes and still seek to dine politically at the master's table in return for a few worthless scraps of the master's food. Rooming in the master's house, their sense of self-respect is stunted under the political weight of the master's roof. They rationalize the failed justification of slavery as historical trivia that is irrelevant to the modern-day social, economic, and political oppression of the African people.

In the language and thinking of their forefathers and foremothers, these house Negroes maintain that those who find themselves unjustly oppressed are justifiably linked to their own inferior stations in life. Spurred by the tenets of conservative patriarchs such as Rush Limbaugh and Dick Cheney, these house Negroes object loudly to accusations that many white conservatives still retain ideas of white supremacy. Indeed, the belief in white dominance as natural and white culture as the harbinger of civilization is a cornerstone of the race supremacy idea among house Negroes. Therefore, as we can see, racism or white racial domination is not merely the philosophy of some whites; it is also the fundamental belief of the black conservatives, the ideological descendants of the house Negroes, who had no problem sustaining the exploitation of Africans in the name of white culture.

Although the memories of Jeffersonian predecessors have withstood the test of time without any hint of tarnish from their moral transgressions, the house Negroes among African folk willfully embrace slavery's shameful past. Beyond the reach of human indignation, they remain psychologically and, thus, politically in a state of human bondage. Their relentless desire to fashion themselves in the current-day master's image is universally acknowledged even if it is never explicitly stated. Similar to antebellum house Negroes, black conservatives fear being relegated to a life of toil among poor and middle-class African Americans should they incur the master's disfavor. In this way, they aspire equally with the master's offspring to live out the American Dream that the signers of the Declaration of Independence first promised to all whites. These black conservatives refuse to admit that the contract with the people of the land was imperfect because it never recognized with any great detail and commitment the need to free Africans from bondage. These modern-day house Negroes are very willing to forget the struggle for freedom engaged in by African Americans who committed themselves to equality and justice. Black conservatives would, however, willingly attribute the liberating spaces that have been found in American society to the generosity of whites—as if struggle was unnecessary. They pay little respect to Nat Turner, Denmark Vesey, Gabriel Prosser, and Harriet Tubman. They are the modern-day house Negroes whose psychological bondage and subsequent apathy are sustained by their politics as the Black Conservative.

—*Molefi K. Asante and Ronald E. Hall*

# CHAPTER ONE

# Slave Psychology

## The Shape of Race Relations

How does a person who is a member of a persecuted group, in the course of oppression, find common cause with the oppressor? The psychology of human bondage is complex, and victims do not cooperate with their captor unless those victims are subjected to some form of violence, either by threat or physical attack. Because humans are naturally opposed to bondage, victims who are subjected to it are thus forced to endure psychological and emotional torment capable of compromising their human spirit in order to tolerate an otherwise unnatural state (Akbar, 1996).

Generally speaking, all people regard themselves, in a normal situation, with pride and self-respect. Africans have participated in kinship respect and ancestral reverence from the earliest of times; in fact, humanity's origin is the African continent. Just like all other people, African people seek life-fulfilling activities. Thus, there are no differences among humans in terms of the enthusiasm for life and the protection of posterity, and few other aspects of the human spirit equal people's innate desire for freedom. Consequently, because freedom is the natural and preferred state of human existence, any attempt to make enslaved Africans of human beings requires that they not only be processed psychologically for what otherwise might be considered an unnatural state of human existence but also that they themselves be forced to cooperate in their own denigration.

Africans who reached America during the European Slave Trade came from people who resisted their enslavement in any way they could. The capture, kidnapping, and imprisoning of Africans in the slave dungeons along Africa's coast were ordeals of criminal magnitude. Often the slave traders would pay Africans to go into the interior to capture young people; most Africans captured for the slave ships were between the ages of 14 and 22. Nothing was assured in these activities: Some victims fought violently and died whereas others succeeded in escape, after killing their capturers. The Africans who were eventually brought to the Americas endured a horrible Atlantic crossing and a naked, dehumanizing, and brutal enslavement (Asante, 2007). In fact, it would not be before the middle of the seventeenth century that British law would require that Africans be clothed.

Europeans altered the slavery formula by classifying people as chattel, as property. Among Africans, there was no history of regarding humans as the property of another. But it was through this notion of human beings as chattel that Europe was able to reduce the African person to something less than a human being in Europe's legal structure. This justification for enslavement was new to the African world, so despite examples of enslavement elsewhere, scholars generally agree that the enslavement of Africans by Europeans was historically unprecedented for Africa.

Slave traders aimed to profit through the bodies of African people, which required the most violent practices in order to break the human spirit so those enslaved might submit willingly to this state of human degradation. Like chattel, Africans were their master's property, given no more rights or privilege than a horse, a cow, or a farmer's pig. In this practice, the African's life purpose was dedicated to serving the master, who might exploit them in any way that served his best interest. Only the most brutal, violent, and omnipotent exercise of power could sustain what was, for all intents and purposes, nothing more than a form of slave psychology. The impact of this slave psychology on the sons and daughters of the house Negroes would, over time, lead to a form of modern-day African American conservatism.

The tenets of this political ideology would not fully emerge until after the campaign for Equal Opportunity led by A. Philip Randolph, the Civil Rights Struggle led by Martin Luther King, Jr., and the Black Power Movement inspired by Malcolm X, Angela Davis, Maulana Karenga, Kwame Ture, Huey Newton, and Bobby Seale, among others. However, it is important to understand how the reactive elements of black conservatism were inherent in these movements. Black conservatives would come to view the liberation efforts of the black community as narrow and shortsighted and would, therefore, posit an approach based on "good American values," by which they always meant following the path of the whites. One can see the emergence of these ideas in historical racist approaches to knowledge.

The effort to influence the African—that is, to make the African a slave and to groom the house Negro—had philosophical antecedents in Europe; it was something grounded in the religion and literature of a great deal of European thought. The English had tried it on the Irish, and the Franks had tried it on the Gauls. However, without apparent reason, blackness itself was viewed as denigration in all facets of Western civilization. Leading European intellectuals such as Hegel and Voltaire expressed their negative opinions about Africans and blackness without critique from their peers. Many Europeans simply accepted that Africans were inferior beings. In fact, Thomas Jefferson, who was deeply influenced by European ideologies, likewise believed in black inferiority.

Furthermore, Christianity may have been the main key to the moral and ethical foundations supporting the enslavement of Africans. It had profited extensively from exploiting enslaved Africans, thereby increasing the wealth of the church and expanding the territory controlled by the church. However, in order to live with such stark contradictions while operating in the name of Jesus Christ, it needed to create the psychological mechanism to justify the exploitation of Africans (Myrdal, 1944). Thus, Christian America eventually aligned itself with pseudo-scientific and religious justifications that described persons of African descent as inferior and/or evil; in fact, because Africans existed in such a state, white intervention was necessary in order to save Africans from themselves. Moreover, as whites sought to maintain a sense of African inferiority, America's first leaders wrote its sacred documents with these intentions in mind. Ultimately, America's earliest institutions justified white exploitation of African people by proclaiming the lofty ideals of white individualism and liberty in one instance while enabling power over and domination of Africans in another (Myrdal, 1944).

As the major American slaveholders practiced Christianity, they also used it to justify killing Native Americans and enslaving Africans. This abuse of Christianity meant that these terrible contradictions would stain the conscience of the founding fathers of the American nation, a mark that would carry the white American ethos into the twenty-first century. Those in power also used Christianity to persecute women, both white and black, who were called witches and burned at the stake during the sixteenth and seventeenth centuries. However, despite the poor media surrounding the persecution of women as witches, this idea of Christianity maintained a firm grasp on all American cultural institutions. Indeed, slavery was the principal activity in which Christianity failed as a moral ideal.

*   *   *

The antebellum South, where African exploitation and brutalization was the most severe, embraced religion to such an extreme so as to psychologically justify its violence against African victims. At that time, white Southerners took their religion so seriously that it came to dominate every aspect of their life, culture, and outward behavior (Myrdal, 1944). White Southerners harbored a deep hatred for Africans, a practice that they often spoke of as the will of God, and this feeling was deeply embedded in the structure of their religion. However, why would God will such horrible crimes against another people—people who were innocent of crimes against their own race? Answers were not necessary, and the propaganda coming from the preachers, priests, editors, scientists, and politicians was so intense that, eventually, white Southerners felt no guilt about the exploitation and degradation of Africans. In fact, the culture of the South and, to some extent, the American population in general used the statements, sermons, reports, and documents of their opinion makers to avoid any inclination toward guilt.

One could reasonably say that the church was the principal institution leading the justification of African enslavement. Where it did not lead, the church was a co-equal partner with the commercial interest in dictating the relationships between whites and blacks. Neither the rebellion of blacks nor the reform movement of the church could end the brutality toward Africans because the ideas justifying African enslavement aggressively pervaded all art forms, institutions, social graces, trivia, and proverbs that constituted white culture. Even soap and food were decorated with negative or pejorative images of Africans.

Although the enslavement of human beings clearly contradicted the teachings of the church, because Europeans found the slave trade profitable, they fashioned a psychology that could alleviate the moral contradiction.

This process would lead to two phenomena: assuaging white guilt and embedding black self-hatred.

White guilt could be eased by applying the concept of *individual free will,* which was first derived from the Protestants during their rebellion against the dominance of the Catholic Church. This concept holds that individuals—and in this case, white individuals—could demonstrate that they were free in relationship to their morality by claiming individual free will. They could do what they pleased, as they pleased, and when they pleased so long as they interpreted it in the context of the Christian doctrine. They did not have to wait for the policy of a church hierarchy that might have thrown them into a quagmire of moral confusion. The clean-cut, precise, and usable "individual free will" could function in ways that many had not even predicted. It was the *sine qua non* of the American slave practice. This was not the case, say, in Brazil or some other nations where the influence of the Catholic Church was omnipotent. In those countries, church hierarchy essentially dictated policies regarding relationships between Africans and Europeans, the care of the enslaved children, the spiritual health of the enslaved, and so forth.

Conversely, Protestantism gave whites the status of free individuals who are no longer dependent on the unifying voice of the church. Africans were outside of this conversation from the beginning, and the fact that enslaving Africans constituted such a serious moral infraction forced the Protestants to seek a resolution by resorting to individual free will. Accordingly, because humans were seen as divine and "God" existed within the individual, people could embrace the practice of slavery while still believing themselves to be moral. Individual freedom became the mantle on which the white American slaveholder could rest his moral concerns. By the authority of his religion, the lone individual became destined, as a white person favored by "God," to rule over the African. Although certain brands of Protestantism more explicitly interpreted this relationship between humans and the divine than others sects, all seemed to define the African as outside of humanity.

It is important to understand that although the Lutheran and Calvinist movements objected to what they considered the abuses of Catholicism, they did not have a more enlightened view about the enslavement of Africans; those branches of Christianity also worked to assuage white guilt over the treatment of Africans. Even though the European enslavement of millions of Africans was unprecedented, Europeans and Arabs had practiced slavery for centuries before the mass forced migration of Africans to the Americas. Thus, when Catholics, Lutherans, Calvinists, and other European Christians began participating in the slave trade in the fifteenth century, they brought to the practice of slavery a unique disregard for the humanity of the enslaved. Although they took part in violence and abuse much as other men did in controlling the enslaved, through their religion and, eventually, science, whites degraded African people as apes, monkeys, or other animals, and they even treated the enslaved worse than they treated animals. The slave master could treat the slaves any way he desired because, from a religious standpoint, Africans had no souls and thus were not included in the laws of God or morality.

The European Renaissance and Industrial Revolution had tremendous impacts on the lives of enslaved African people in the American South. During the late Renaissance, the sixteenth and early seventeenth centuries, European society was transformed by centralizing political institutions and world exploration. In a sense, the people had been freed from fears stoked by the ruling religious hierarchies of the European Middle Ages.

The Renaissance had given Europeans a vehicle through which to pursue activities gratifying to both soul and body, responding to both abstraction and physicality. The Industrial Revolution, emerging in the eighteenth and nineteenth centuries, would encourage the development of factories to manufacture goods created or harvested by enslaved Africans. The changes brought about by these two movements were so revolutionary that European governments would create new money and opportunities, often without consideration for long-established, traditional practices and beliefs. Individuals were granted permission to seek whatever goals they desired for personal benefit, which contrasted the sternness imposed by the era of Luther and Calvin. Even if American whites seldom acknowledged that their romantic attitudes of individual liberty and democracy grew out of European ideas grounded in individualism, when one understands how individual free will allowed the most decadent form of individualism, the truth becomes inescapable. As noted African scholar W. E. B. Du Bois has stated, "it was the freedom to destroy freedom, the freedom of some to exploit the rights of others" (Dubois, 1939, p. 127). Indeed, this individualism permitted freedom to be intolerant and to cast the collective interests of society to hell. Hence, in the reality of the antebellum South, because the white man was determined to be free, he, despite contradiction, felt entitled by race to enslave and otherwise oppress African people.

This invasive individualism, exploitative and avaricious, would also transform all rights into individual rights. Supported by the legal systems of the state, institutionalized individualism sought to make collective identities illegal, marginal, and fictional. Thus, each entity was recognized legally as an individual, whether it were a business or a not-for-profit organization, and black people, as descendants of enslaved persons, were transformed legally into isolated cells to be picked off at will by the more aggressive ideological individualist.

Furthermore, Christian ideology, with its good and evil dichotomy constructed to maintain white superiority and black inferiority, affected deeply the psychology of the African. In fact, it can be argued that when slavery began, no African believed him or herself inferior to Europeans. Instead, Africans believed themselves to be unfortunate. African cultures and civilizations were often older, more developed, and more stable than those of Europeans. Because of this, whites must have exerted a remarkable amount of effort to embed such self-hatred in people whose ancestors had tamed incredible territories by bringing those lands under the plow and hoe as well as making iron and refining gold long before whites came to Africa. Enslavement was itself the first stage to self-hatred.

How can a people whose freedom had never been questioned and whose liberties as African citizens had been ensured by their constitutions be made to doubt the worth of their own selves? What methods of indoctrination must be practiced to gain entry into the psyche of Africans to the extent that they would claim they had no knowledge when indeed they descend from a tradition that is known for creating knowledge? Or who would deny that they had institutions of higher learning when there were several schools that taught the higher disciplines in West Africa? What could make a beautiful person accustomed to being ornamented in fine jewelry and clothes claim that Africans had no clothes and no jewelry? What form of human torture must be used to cause the African to lose these memories? There has to be, if not a physical waterboarding, a psychological waterboarding of tsunami proportions.

From the moment a slave hunter captured an African boy or girl, man or woman, he led that African away from the village and down to the coast to be placed in dungeons to wait for the arrival of the European slaving ship, which could take months. There, the slave captors deprived the African of his or her own thoughts and began the process of brainwashing. There were several aspects to this early stage of making a slave. First, the person was made to believe that there was something wrong with him or her because they had been captured whereas the Africans who were working cooperatively with the white man were not somehow wrong. Captured people could see other Africans in the service of the whites at the dungeons, and they knew that some of these Africans were from ethnic groups that were different from their own. Such knowledge probably made them believe that there was something wrong with their group, and this was why they were the ones captured and held in bondage. Secondly, the captors exposed the captives to Christianity, making them listen to Christian hymns even as the whites abused them. There was always something quite odd about the nature of the enslavement when sad dirges of pain would mix with the Christian songs coming from the church. The shock of these differences and the uncertainty of one's fate must have been the cruelest actions against the psychological health of the captives. One was outside of the power of one's own king or queen, separated from one's own mother or father, concealed from the searching spirits of the ancestors, and abandoned by one's named god. Clearly, one was now in the hands of a monster that could bring about the most horrible of deaths, could eat you, leaving no traces that could be tracked by your loved ones.

Crossing the ocean in a small boat, with nearly 800 people packed tightly together for a 30- to 60-day journey, was the gate of hell. In response to this experience, the African would question existence and divinity. However, whereas some accepted existence and divinity, others accepted only divinity, and still others, the more rational thinkers, accepted existence. In our judgment, the fact that Africans could not see the contradictions inherent in a system of cruel oppression practiced by white slave holders and, later, their own reliance on the same Christian god is another gate to hell. It was the opening the slave masters needed to destroy Africans' self-confidence and erase their memory.

By 1600 the system for assuaging white guilt and blaming the African had been firmly established. Spaniards and Portuguese were among the first and most organized Europeans to set up trade mechanisms with Africans and build forts from which to conduct their business. After a hundred years of kidnapping and trading in African people as chattel, whites began to consider African enslavement as normal and, in turn, looked for new more profitable ways to exploit them.

The potential wealth from slavery prompted Europeans to consider the question of who among them should be licensed to trade in human cargo. This consideration was a reflection of the emerging competition and the significance of slave traffic to economic power. To reach such a state, Christianity had soundly rationalized slavery as justified. To rescue the white psyche, the Portuguese and Spaniards then organized missionary trips to Africa and elsewhere to save heathen native peoples from themselves. In this way, whites could claim the support of God and thus psychologically justify what they were doing. If they raped and pillaged African civilizations, it was not for selfish interests but rather a divine inspiration supported by both God and the king. Whites would enlist the church as one of the arbiters of licenses, called *asientos,* that would ensure a certain nation or trading company the right to search for captives in a certain area of Africa without fear of competition from other nations or companies. The asiento was paid to the Catholic Church and the Spanish king and was based on the number of Africans ripped from the land. Because it gave a company or nation the rights to the area for up to 30 years, the asiento was considered a prized possession because it almost ensured wealth. Those who held the asiento also had the right to trade it to another power, so selling asientos was a profitable business as well.

Although, beginning in 1501, the first Africans brought to the Americas were enslaved on Hispaniola, the island that was divided between Haiti and Dominican Republic, Africans were not brought to the English Colony of Virginia until 1619. By this time, the philosophy supporting enslavement was deeply rooted in the white psyche, and the codes, sometimes called Black Codes, had been written, describing the nature of the relationship between Africans and whites. It is also interesting to note that around this time Zumba Ganga was leading the Palmares Republic in Brazil. Even though Virginia and the other North American British colonies may have been late to the monstrous business of slave trading, they entered it with the intention of becoming the leading slaving nation. While the first twenty Africans were indentured in Jamestown, Virginia—joining the status of Africans in the Spanish-controlled parts of the Americas, such as Florida, South Carolina, and what became Arizona and New Mexico—the first

American attempt to stigmatize African people by race also occurred in the slave state of Virginia. Before the 1660s, both Africans and whites could be indentured, but soon the Virginia legislature passed a law requiring all people of the "African race" to be held in bondage in perpetuity. Thus, in one swift move, the term *race* entered the lexicon of enslavement along with perpetual African slavery.

In the history of American civilization, especially the South, Christianity often assumed the status of science. That is, whatever phenomena it deemed as truth and fact could not be challenged without accusation of sin or evil. Christians argued that it was sinful for whites to marry Africans because Africans were heathens. Nevertheless, the sinners went about raping any black woman in their "possession" because she was property. Sin abounded in the South as it did everywhere else, and these Christians explained the intellectual contortions necessary to sustain the ideology of racism by referencing the Bible. For example, they assumed that the people in the Bible were whites and that for a white man to marry a woman from the land of Nod, a civilization dated older than the Biblical Adam, he would be deemed immoral because the Nodites were by all accounts Africans (Rogers, 1957).

Today, many of these representations of Africans provoke pity or laughter from scientists or intelligent readers of history. However, early American literature abounds with astonishing tales of Africans, such as the beast in the *Book of Revelations*, tales that white Americans took as fact. What's more, the white psychological domination of enslaved Africans was so extensive that many blacks also came to believe the biblical tales depicting African people as nonhuman. They embraced this racialized form of biblical interpretation to such an extent that they rejected the possibility that Africans could be considered good enough to be chosen by the Christian god. By the time the whites had woven their psychological domination deeply in the fabric of American social thought, they had also, even if in a less perfect form, entwined their spiritual control into the psyche of the African who had accepted Christianity. The Bible was an infallible source, and those who quoted its scriptures in their teaching to impressionable African congregations emphasized "servants had to obey their masters." When Africans accepted precepts and ideas such as this, they had no chance to rebound from the psychological domination that the enslavers set in place.

Perhaps the most devastating narrative of negativity about Africans is the biblical story of Ham, in which the negative portrayal of blackness is often utilized to rationalize the enslavement of Africans. In this way, slaveholders used the Bible and Christian mythology to attempt to dehumanize African people. Through these biblical and cultural myths, Africans were effectively demonized as those who were meant to be slaves. This line of thinking persisted even though most authorities believe that the word slave is derived from the word Slav because it related to the bondage of the ancestors of the Slavic people. Notwithstanding that fact, whites utilized the tale of Noah and his three sons, Shem, Japhet, and Ham—which was originally taken from the Jewish texts—in order to impact profoundly the white psyche regarding ideas of race. These ideas would be further solidified in the practice of slavery in the South. By associating Africans with Ham, whites provided a convenient mechanism for demonstrating that Africans had no paternal relationship to the divine and were meant to be hewers of wood and servants forever. The rejection of Ham's descendants then represents, according to Christian mythology, the retaliatory castration by the higher father in god. What was banished or rejected would not be seen in a Freudian sense, or as when King Oedipus was said to have blinded and banished himself for learning what he had done with his mother. Rather, after punishing one among their number, Noah's remaining sons then earned the approval and protection of God, their paternal Father. This narrative, therefore, represented the cultural absorption of the exceptional nature of whiteness as it also further contributed to a negative association with dark skin. Here, the bad and evil son, set apart from humanity by the curse of dark skin, had been forever banished from the acceptable fold of humanity until the European descendants of the white sons of Noah discovered him again—in Africa (Rogers, 1957).

Eventually Western scholars sought to scientifically rationalize the story of Ham. They first attempted to account for dark and/or African skin by proposing that it was due to the intense sun in the African region, but this hypothesis did not last very long because there were Native Americans on similar latitudes who were lighter skinned than Africans. Many learned people utilized the myth of Ham to account for what could not be substantiated scientifically. Subsequently, Europeans, enabled by psychodynamics, inculcated the view that the bodies of the dark-skinned peoples of Africa were the manifestation of the most primal of curses on humankind. These assumptions formed the bases for many of the later sexual fantasies surrounding race. However, although such fantasies had not incorporated the abstract concept of race until the advent of the European slave trade, they further encouraged justification for enslaving Africans. The advent of the European Slave Trade and Western colonization brought about numerous social and psychosocial fantasies pertaining to blackness, particularly when associated with dark-skinned people. Thus, in the Western world, a racial mythology developed where dark-skinned people—Africans in particular—represented the embodiment of negativity, sexuality, ignorance, and obscenity.

Freud developed theoretical principles to analyze these ideas of the struggle of light against darkness, of whites assaulting blackness, and of the necessity of positing something as good against something else as bad. Freud's practice of psychoanalysis theorized that the ego is motivated by the super-ego, which is the good and moral influence, and the id, which is something not seen and is associated with darkness—that is, blackness, black skin, black people. Luther and Calvin had already laid the foundations for this abstraction, so the ground was prepared for racists to use it later to explain enslavement. Thus, the id represents blackness within the personality. Its underlying components, repressed from consciousness, reveal themselves symbolically vis-à-vis fantasies of race. Of course, Freud lived long after the enslavement, but his theories are useful to make sense of the dichotomy between blackness and whiteness in the human psyche, as exploited by whites during slavery.

Using Freud's psychodynamics of blackness, we can see how Western civilization had revealed its own psychological structure by what it was projecting onto dark-skinned people. Christianity had assumed the task of being a direct representative of the culture that destroyed African civilization, thus necessitating missionary assistance for Africans. The dual role of this assistance makes it an appropriate sacrifice, in the blackness myth, to the more barbaric entity that it serves. Thus, having wedged itself securely into the Western psyche, dark skin, seen as spiritual blackness, dominated as the focus of human degradation. Psychodynamically, Western culture had found a way to resolve—through projection—much of its color conflicts at the expense of dark-skinned people. It was a convenient justification for slavery. Vis-à-vis the myth of race, the "white" man was now psychologically free—that is without guilt—to exploit Africans and other dark-skinned people. As a result, the unconscious oedipal drives could be symbolically acted out in real life without inhibition. The antebellum maternal figure was then divided into the pure "white" mother and the impure, lustful "black" *mammy*. The "black" man represented both the bad father to be castrated and the bad son—Ham—to be castrated as punishment for castrating his father—Noah. What's more, he is the aim of projected oedipal desires for the antebellum "white" mother. The "black" woman also became a sexually available object for repressed "white" oedipal desires for the mother while at the same time she symbolized lust (Hall, 2003).

This complex rationale was the model from which white Christian racists for centuries would psychologically shape the eventual appearance of the Black Conservative, who, by force of psychological domination, would become a self-loathing black who would see more value in white ancestry than in African, more glory in white history than African, and more appreciation in white art, music, and literature than in African. We are not the first to declare that the African in America has been miseducated. Carter G. Woodson, the father of African American History, wrote *The Mis-education of the Negro* in 1933. Some of the titles of the chapters of this famous book offer a glimpse into Woodson's perspective, as can be seen by the following: "The Seat of the Trouble," "How We Missed the Mark," "How We Drifted Away from the Truth," "Education Under Outside Control," "The Failure to Learn to Make a Living," "The Educated Negro Leaves the Masses," "Dissension and Weakness," "Professional Educated Discouraged," "Political Education Neglected," "The Loss of Vision," "The Need for Service Rather than Leadership," "Hirelings in the Place of Public Servants," "Understand the Negro," "The New Program," "Vocational Guidance," "The Type of Professional Man Required," "Higher Strivings in the Service of the Country," and "The Study of the Negro." What Woodson observed was that African Americans had been dislocated by the teachings of the schools and churches. The idea that blacks were the children of Ham had conditioned Africans to accept a lower status. Thus, the Ham narrative tainted everything, producing in both whites and blacks a negativity regarding Africans that continues to this day. This narrative was a justificatory instrument meant primarily for the destruction of blackness as valuable, and can even be seen when, in twentieth-century apartheid, among factions of the South African Dutch Reform Church, the story of Ham justified colonialism. Hence, religion produced myths that were the basis for a system of oppression. Of course, because whites taught or otherwise created the teaching documents for blacks, Africans also believed in this doctrine of white privilege vis-à-vis the African. Bantu Stephen Biko once said at a rally that when white police officers found a black who seemed promising as a black police officer, they would ask him to arrest his own mother. If the black man was so convinced of his inferiority and the rightness of the whites, he would bring his mother to the police station. Thus, the myths meant to alleviate guilt for whites likewise affected the sense of self-worth for many blacks.

Although various European scientists pursued the issue of race from various vantage points, all arrived at traditional outcomes that associated Africans with inferiority. One such scientist, Peter Camper (1722–1789), a professor of anatomy at Groningen in the Netherlands, designed what became known as Camper's facial angle, which measured physiognomic dimensions. Camper calculated this angle by observing the human head in a profile position. This was one of the first instances of Western scientific research that utilized objective instruments to supposedly measure racial criteria. When used properly, the instruments could assumingly calculate the similarity of a human head to an animal head. In European history, Africans were thought to have the smallest facial angle relative to their heads, thus making them the lowest racial group within the human species (Richards, 1997). Although he opposed slavery, Camper nevertheless believed that his calculations proved that blacks were closer to animals than whites. Other scientists, according to Pieterse, in their quest to establish the first scientific classification of mankind, subsequently utilized Camper's work. In the scientific description of Ethiopians, that is, blacks, the following accounts stigmatized blackness and validated the acceptance of this stigma as a common cultural norm in Western civilization, one that was then carried over and inculcated in America as a common cultural norm:

> Ethiopian variety: colour black, hair African and curly, head narrow, compressed at the sides; forehead knotty, uneven, molar bones protruding outwards; eyes very prominent; nose thick, mixed up as it were with the wide jaws; alveolar edge narrow, elongated in front; upper primaries obliquely prominent; lips very puffy; chin retreating. Many are bandy-legged. To this variety belong all the Africans, except those of the north. (Pieterse, 1992, pp. 34–37)

By the time of the American Declaration of Independence in 1776, slavery had been firmly established in the Americas. During the Constitutional Convention, the framers of the Constitution determined that the slave trade should be outlawed across the sea by 1807; however, domestic slavery was not limited. By the time the new nation under the Constitution was born, there were a million enslaved Africans in the United States. It is significant to note that although slavery had begun to decline in the North, it continued to increase as a way of life in the South, where dominant white group privilege was tied to human bondage. The North was, thus, in a position to claim moral high ground, where dependency on slavery was hardly an option. The South, likely no less moral, relied on slavery to support its economy, and for this reason, it used every means available, including psychological manipulation, to justify it.

The issue of slavery became a source of tension between the North and South and eventually culminated in the Civil War. In the aftermath of war between the northern and southern states, slavery was then brought to an end not for reasons of humanity but in an effort to preserve the Union. Unfortunately, ending slavery did not end the struggles of African folk to overcome their systemic and institutionalized cultural degradation.

In the postslavery era, the African American, that is, African, population increased, making it at the time the largest non-European racial group in America. Unfortunately, gaining physical and legal freedom did not significantly improve the quality of African American life because racism, the active institutional discrimination of black people, and the continuing psychological impact of slavery continued into the twenty-first century. In fact, discrimination, prejudice, and various forms of violence inflicted by post–Civil War southern whites sustained a slave class among blacks immediately after 1877, the end of Reconstruction, and this went on while most whites in Northern states looked on with little more than apathy and dismay until the Civil Rights Movement of the 1960s. Despite violence and intimidation, however, many blacks improved their lives through hard struggle and dedication to excellence in their work. Scientists, artists, scholars, teachers, and businessmen and women sought to create avenues of progress for the masses of blacks. The number of former enslaved Africans who could read and write steadily increased, and by 1915 more than half of the black population was literate. This was a phenomenal achievement. Walter White, the legendary leader of the NAACP during the early to mid-twentieth century, declared that blacks had achieved literacy more rapidly than citizens of many European nations that had never had slavery.

Expectedly in a racist society, the mulatto class, counted in the censuses of 1850, 1860, 1870, and 1890, made dramatic gains in population. Their numbers, according to these censuses, were considerable and contradicted the socially constructed myth of race. In 2008 Henry Louis Gates estimated that nearly one out of every seven African Americans has white ancestry. Thus, one could see that the structure of American society helped to generate this mulatto population at the turn of the twentieth century, and this was especially true in the South, where even after slavery, whites tended to have absolute power over the black family. Attempts to calculate the precise numbers of mulattoes are no doubt subject to error and/or miscalculation. Nevertheless, some general results have been obtained that suggest that from 11 to 16 percent of those classifying themselves as African at the time had some amount of white ancestry (Franklin, 1969). Although there are some exceptions, many mulattoes operated as the psychological, social, and political extension of the white master class. These mulattoes expected that, because they were lighter skinned, their lives would be better and that they could advance more readily than a darker-skinned black person, even though the masses of black people were still oppressed and segregated.

The existence of mixed-race African Americans—in particular those having white blood—confounded the politicians, scientists, and social planners of the American South. In an era dominated by racial ideologies that extolled the virtues of white supremacy and African inferiority, mixed-blood African Americans stood as testimony of the white failure to retain the notion of white purity. These mulattoes, the offspring of whites and blacks, had to be given up to the black community: When whiteness was constructed as a purity of race, mulattoes could not possibly be accepted as white. In order to sustain group privilege and justify African subordination, white Americans continued to define membership in the African race via "one-drop theory," which maintained that any citizen owing even "one drop" of their racial heritage to African blood would be counted as African (Franklin, 1969). Furthermore, no mainstream scientist of that time questioned the pseudoscience of what determined the measure of "one drop." The ultimate goal, therefore, was to compromise mixed race blacks and utilize the construct of race to define and/or rationalize persons with any degree of African descent as inferior and not suited for the privileges and opportunities normally extended to white American citizens. This action created a tenacious racism that served to rationalize the disproportionate distribution of wealth and resources to members of dominant white race groups. Thus, the worth of racial myths increased via the practical application of racist acts committed by such groups against all blacks, even those with white paternity.

When pressed, most white Americans will acknowledge the socioeconomic origin of African oppression. They are quite aware that before Columbus discovered America in 1492 and before the slave trade, racism was not a major problem. When the Spaniards took the advice of Bartholomew las Casas to replace Native Americans with Africans, they set in motion an entire train of African enslavement that would eventually lead to justifications for slavery that were rooted in physical appearances.

W. E. B. Du Bois, the greatest African American scholar of the twentieth century, preached the economic origins of race prejudice. However, he contended that through the longevity of economic privilege, given the negative portrayal of blacks, there gradually evolved an American social and racial folklore imbued with the idea of white superiority. This American social and racial folklore superimposed racism onto the general fabric of white racial behavior and led to whites' willingness to exploit blacks as a means to maintain a privileged way of life for whites while subjecting blacks to the worst types of segregation and social discrimination. By embracing this folklore, whites' ability to sense what was fair and just in a democratic society eventually dulled. In the aftermath of slavery, limited Reconstructions, Jim Crow laws, and economic deprivation, most Americans were not alarmed by how racist American consciousness had become (Franklin, 1969). Regardless to the depth of racist thinking, which also infected popular culture, toys, memorabilia, and consumer products, white Americans lost sight of racism's pervasiveness even as they were in the midst of it. In effect, racism was buried so far into their subconscious that they lost the ability to comprehend it as a social problem. African American psychologists such as Wade Nobles, Asa Hilliard, and Na'im Akbar have articulated a theory of racism that posits it as a social pathology, not so much for blacks as for whites. Although many scholars have studied racism's effects on blacks over the past couple of decades, even more researchers, following the early work of Benjamin Bowser and his associates, look at its impact on whites. Fortunately, in spite of the overwhelming racist environment in which they have had to work, thinkers such as Joe Feagin, Tim Wise, and others have challenged the orthodoxy and discovered the degree to which racism has permeated the fabric of American culture (Kovel, 1984).

Akin to slave psychology, the contemporary negative image of African people lives on in the symbolism of America's various institutions. One of the oldest myths in popular American culture is the good guy–bad guy dichotomy in which the bad guys always dress in black. No doubt, racists alone did not create the symbols that connect Africans with bad or evil; however, racists cultivated existing psychological associations with blackness that are pervasive and extend deeply into the American cultural psyche. For example, when anyone suffers a terrible misfortune at a given point in time, Americans—both black and white—still refer to it as a "black day." During the Depression years, the term *Black Thursday* became a part of common language. Anyone who commits a heinous act will "blacken" his or her reputation, and then others may persecute them by "blacklisting," "blackballing," or "blackmailing" them (Kovel, 1984). As a case in point, the Chicago White Sox baseball team was "blackballed" in the 1919 World Series for deliberately losing to profit in gambling. For a while thereafter, they were referred to as the Chicago Black Sox, and to this day the "Black Sox Scandal" is universally considered a "dark" chapter in American sports history. However, these negative implications of "black" extend far beyond baseball, as suggested by boxing great Muhammad Ali. According to Ali, the fact that Americans refer to white cake as "angel food cake" and dark cake as "devil's food cake" is not a coincidence (Williams, 1964).

Common American expressions, as harmless as they seem, play a vital role in the psychological strategy to denigrate African people and to shape what would become the Black Conservative. The negative implications of "African" in the general population and "black" among African American themselves started with religion and were then validated by so-called scientists in their research on the significance of skin color. According to one experiment that used college students and seventh graders, the results were not surprising. When asked to make semantic differential ratings of colors, both groups associated "black" with evil, death, and badness (Williams, 1964). What's more, this association between black and evil is not strictly an American phenomenon; college students in Germany, Denmark, Hong Kong, and India make similar associations (Williams and McMurty, 1970). Even more astounding is the fact that ethnic groups in Central Africa have similar tendencies (Williams, Moreland, and Underwood, 1970)! The research of Adams and Osgood (1973) further revealed the pervasiveness of this universal association of blackness with negativity. However, such researchers have often failed to acknowledge that blackness as a concept relates to dark skin color. Although cultures may associate "blackness" with evil and, therefore, argue that African people are evil, the same logic does not apply to Africans themselves, who see blackness as purity, stability, the origin of humanity, beauty, as well as a color. This is why one of the oldest adages in the African American community, despite that the concept behind it struggles to take root psychologically, is "the blacker the berry, the sweeter the juice."

By focusing the negativity associated with blackness in science and religion and realizing the potential for slave profit, whites psychologically prepared an element of the African population to eventually oppose itself. That element tolerated brutality and moral contradiction, which enabled whites to further exploit African people. According to Gunnar Myrdal (1944), a pioneer in race studies, the central problem was not the exploitation of blacks nor the resulting effects of this exploitation in America, but rather it was the moral compromises that otherwise decent white Americans made that impacted those accommodating blacks (Myrdal, 1944). Yet it is clear that racism was profoundly and deeply unsettling to black people, the primary victims of white brutality and oppression. We do not deny the fact that whites were affected; in fact, we agree with Myrdal that these moral compromises have been real and troubling in the white American psyche. White Americans' attempt to construct conceptual conduits between the egalitarian creed of liberty, freedom, and justice for all while attempting to dehumanize the African was an astounding and formidable feat that could not have been sustained without some element of African cooperation. In order to illuminate the problem, we must understand in a political context the role of the African in sustaining white oppression of the masses of Africans. Almost no sector of society, economics, social welfare, law, housing, or education escapes the insidious and vile attacks on African people.

In particular, education has always been a chaotic battlefield for culture. One simply has to look to the struggles for Afrocentric schools in New York, Philadelphia, Chicago, Detroit, and Washington to see how bitterly whites have opposed the idea that all students should have an education that grounds them in their own culture. The American educational system has aimed to wipe the African clean of any iota of Africanity. Furthermore, in many ways African educators have been compliant as African and African American culture has been destroyed as they have maintained a white supremacist structure of education as the desired outcome of Americanization. Conversely, educators such as Asa Hilliard, Susan Goodwin, Ellen Schwartz, Wade Nobles, Joyce King, and Ama Mazama have created curricula and infused African content into their teaching, and their work has made significant strides to stop the obliteration of African history and culture (Asante and Mazama, 2010, pp. 12–23).

Southern whites often made reference to "custom" or "the old school" as reasons to tolerate the degradation of and economic discrimination against African people. This same notion can be seen in the history of racial differences in teacher salaries in the southern states:

> An additional argument in favor of the salary differential is the general tradition of the South that blacks and whites are not to be paid equivalent salaries for equivalent work. The attitude may be considered wrong from whatever angle it is viewed, but the fact remains that the custom is one that is almost universal and one that the practical school administrator must not ignore. (Adams and Osgood, 1973, p. 135)

Thus, even the most morally fit southern white failed to object effectively to such injustices. Southern whites' upheld a simple contention: "what was and is, shall be and ought to be" was the order of the day (Myrdal, 1944). Ironically, Myrdal reported that southern whites seldom if ever defended the degradation of black people on the basis of their own economic gain, but such gain was, nevertheless, clearly the sole reasoning behind their tolerance. But he also found that some blacks thought similarly, perhaps because they too, as Southerners, had been subjected to the same psychological, religious, and scientific traditions as white folk. Myrdal discovered that, when pressed, the most cooperative black person would resort to statements such as "This is a white man's country." In a similar vein, they might contend that "We don't have money enough to pay our white workers decent wages," or in an effort to appear rational to a perceived white audience, they will state, "The appropriations do not suffice even to give the white children good schools" (Myrdal, 1944).

Although people who are more consciously accepting likely interpret these prior statements as appalling, the psychologically dominated black person would not be the least disturbed. Through this type of mind-bending, as seen by Myrdal and others since, some blacks accept the downward spiral toward reactionary positions. For example, southern society honored Robert E. Lee, the general who commanded the Confederate Army, and expressed that veneration by naming children, both white and black, after him. When a parent assigns a child either the last or the middle name "Lee," this act was clearly capable of making an ordinary African think that the world was white. Thus, black parents named their children "Mamie Lee," "Arthur Lee," "Johnnie Lee," "Carol Lee," "Willie Lee," and so forth to indicate their Southern, though not necessarily Confederate, sympathies. If we disregard surnames, we still find that from 1870 to 1970, between 10 and 20 percent of southern blacks, had the middle name "Lee." This mental cruelty continued unabated in this regard until the 1960s and 1970s, when black American intellectuals and conscious youth rejected "slave names." However, we hasten to add that black people's response to oppression is no different from the response of other people to similar facts.

This example demonstrates that many Africans considered themselves wards of the white people. They could easily say, after freedom had come, that "We should leave that to Mr. Lester," or "Mr. Williams will handle that," or "We have to ask Mr. Smith for such-and-such." These sentiments reflect a consciousness of people who have lost their own sense of agency or who have been down so long that they do not see any way out of the situation except to call the white man. Assuming the British notion that the world was "the white man's burden," southern whites believed—and blacks accepted this until the 1950s antisegregation protests—that black people can't live without the aid and assistance of some white person. Many critics have even argued that the recently popular movie *Avatar* continues to reinforce the mentality that oppressed people must wait for the "white" savior. In fact, this theme prevails in American films, as can also be seen in *The Last Samurai*.

Thus, the trick is to obtain surreptitiously the approval of black people themselves. In another example, Khari Davis, a young teenager, repeated the famous Doll Test created by Kenneth and Mamie Clark that demonstrated how, even by the middle of the twentieth century, young black children preferred white dolls to black (M. K. Asante, Jr., 2008). Davis discovered that black children, even in 2005, continued to choose the white doll over the black because they perceived it as the "good" doll. In effect, these black children had accepted the society's indoctrination about whiteness. Consequently, although there is evidence that Myrdal's findings would be somewhat different today given the long struggle for equality in society, there are still black people who maintain at any cost an intense dislike of blackness and a great love for whiteness.

The doctrine of white superiority is often clandestine and sophisticated. For instance, there is a common argument that blacks do not need as much as whites to live. In fact, blacks can sustain themselves on much less than what the average white person spends. In South Africa and Zimbabwe, whites, once they heard that the wages of blacks were going to be raised, exclaimed that "blacks do not need much to get along." White Americans made this same argument in the 1940s about African American wages. Apparently, whites marveled at Africans' ability to survive with the small about of money they received (Myrdal, 1944, pp. 35–72). In contrast, this belief contradicted previous notions that blacks were reckless consumers. Southern whites, however, selectively overlooked this gross distortion of facts and refused to recognize yet another contradiction of justice, liberty, and equality: "the cost-of-living and the standard-of-living arguments" (Myrdal, 1944, pp. 74–80). The former of these culturally sanctioned beliefs can be seen in the previously mentioned university study. Furthermore, Myrdal also documented the presence of this belief, citing the following quote:

> observation alone would suggest to the unbiased observer that the Negro teacher will be able to purchase within her society a relatively higher standard of living than the white teacher will be able to secure with the same amount of money. (1944, p. 217)

The rampant discrimination against African Americans as a cultural norm meant that black teachers, having no other choice, spent less money on cost-of-living items because they were paid less than white teachers for the same work. In turn, southern whites used that fact to justify paying blacks less, regardless of the fact that they got along on less has nothing whatsoever to do with the fact that they lived on less. Instead, they had no other choice despite that the cost of living might dictate spending more.

Regardless of the absurdity of reasoning, it was common among southern whites and some blacks without regard to their levels of education. The ignorant as well as the learned accepted this circular reasoning as truth because their quality of life, their economic well-being, was contingent on its acceptance. Thus, by way of the slave psychology through the religious and scientific negation of African people, the genesis of black conservatism is represented ideally in the political life of the well-known accommodationist, Booker T. Washington.

Booker T. Washington was the light-skinned offspring of a slave master born out of the rape of his African chattel. Psychologically, Washington was an exact political extension of his white conservative father. However, it is important to note that white Americans held a different view of blacks such as Washington. Myrdal found that whites' felt increasing antagonism toward all blacks who stepped "out of their place," and this made whites less inclined to distinguish between light and dark African Americans (Myrdal, 1944, pp. 23–29). This is why they felt pleased with exceptions such as Booker T. Washington. Washington represented a large portion of the psychologically dominated, light-skinned African middle class, whom he felt should ignore racism and rescue themselves from their justified white denigration by pursuing economic prosperity through professional occupations. In the 1890s those for and against Washington's principles drew their political lines in the sand. The leader's severest critics came from the faculties of Virginia Union, Atlanta, and Fisk Universities (Franklin, 1969). As a result, Washington exposed a political schism that had been growing for some time in the African community between those who submitted to white denigration of blackness and those who resisted it. Despite that whites supported Washington, his prestige grew and he was eventually regarded as the outstanding exponent of black industrial education. He advocated industrial education because he thought disagreeing with whites over whites' belief that blacks were intellectually inferior was futile. However, his own people increasingly opposed his arguments (Franklin, 1969, pp. 167–190). As tensions escalated between the various factions, opponents hurled charges and counter charges at each other. Blacks who resisted the negative characterizations of African people represented the interests of the masses and could not understand the reasoning of the often light-skinned African conservative power group, which included professionals, educators, "in" politicians, and administrators (Kronus, 1971). Blacks who fought the degrading of Africans did not understand Washington's supporters because these black conservatives operated from a white frame of reference. Washington manifested this frame of reference in his life and works, demonstrating himself to be a biological and spiritual personification of slave psychology who came to shape modern-day black conservatism.

# CHAPTER TWO

# Field Negroes and House Negroes

European settlers saw America primarily as a land for farming. However, they faced two overwhelming obstacles when farming in the American colonies: claiming the land from the Native Americans and clearing the forestlands. The Europeans met the first obstacle with their guns and the second with the influx of enslaved Africans. Initially, whites used enslaved Africans to clear the land and also to serve as buffers between whites and Native Americans. Indeed, Lerone Bennett sees Africans as being used ironically to introduce Christianity to Native Americans, and this activity became the realm of the field Negroes in the earliest American colonies (Bennett, 2007, pp. 18–38).

Most Africans were field Negroes. There was no special characteristic that defined one as a field Negro other than the need for labor on certain projects. Thus, those who may have been identified as house Negroes could, in special cases, be used as field Negroes. However, it was rare that a field Negro would be entrusted with house duties unless he or she had been observed to be particularly hard on other enslaved persons. For instance, a head Negro whose job it was to keep others in line and to report deviations from the master's instructions could be employed in specific duties around the big house. For the most part, field Negroes never left the fields or factories.

Africans were taken from hundreds of ethnic groups along the coast of the continent. Some groups specialized in rice farming, others in indigo, others in growing maize, and some in deep-sea fishing, blacksmithing, and other industries. Nevertheless, when the Mandinka, Wolof, Serere,

Kongo, Yoruba, Igbo, Ewe, Ga, Dan, Hausa, Asante, Akyem, Fante, and other groups landed in the Caribbean and North America, they were used as field Negroes, regardless of their special skills and talents.

## Preparing the Field Negro

Europeans engaged in the slave trade as a business venture because wealth determined their sense of worth. Subsequently, when Europeans transported Africans to the Americas, it was always done in such a way as to maximize the value of the captives. No cost was spared to ensure that Africans were delivered in good condition to the slave ports in the Americas (Haley, 1996, pp. 11–58). All decisions made were in the interest of profit. For instance, if there was a lack of water or food, then the slave ship captain would purge some of his ship's cargo by throwing overboard a number of Africans to save others for the slave markets. Some traders thought that to ensure a fairly good chance of having a workable number of Africans to gain large profits, the ship should start its voyage with too many Africans. Because many would die in the crossing, to make a large profit, one needed a surplus of Africans in order to safely transport enough slaves to market after many others perished. Other traders tried transporting smaller numbers but with more food and water, hoping in the process to reduce the number of deaths while delivering healthy and strong Africans to the market for higher sales and, thus, greater profit. However, nothing could guarantee the health of the human cargo, and therefore, European companies were established to insure the investments of the wealthy individuals who had hired the captains and crews to outfit the slavers for them. Human beings were the gold, the cotton, the petroleum, the rubber, the salt, the nuclear energy of the day; every institution in the European world was involved in one way or another in helping the operators maximize the potential for profit. Capturing and transporting Africans was an expensive undertaking, but the European person or company willing to take the risk could also reap a substantial profit.

Conditions on slave ships were often unfit for human habitat. In fact, slave merchants likely gave better care to animals being transported for sale. Enslaved Africans, however, were frequently crammed into spaces on slave ships much too small to accommodate their bodies. They had no access to facilities to relieve themselves, and thus, might lay for the entire voyage in their own feces and urine. Menstruating women had no way to care for themselves. Food and water were rationed to each captive in portions just large enough to keep them alive long enough to arrive at port. In most cases, a certain number of Africans were expected to die as a consequence of the conditions, rebellion, and murderous discipline. Some Africans committed suicide whereas others drank their own urine and tasted feces in an effort to stave off the pain of hunger. When death took hold, their bodies were simply thrown overboard to be eaten by sharks. Those who completed the voyage were the forerunners of the enslaved population. Having endured such a treacherous and brutal undertaking, they had shown themselves to be sturdy of body and of sound enough mind to function as field and house Negroes. Men and women were equally strong, having survived the same brutal voyage.

When the slave ships landed in the Americas, usually the West Indies, Africans were taken and "seasoned" by slave overseers noted for their ability to "make a slave." These seasoning farms were the sites of cruelties unknown to the civilized Africans who did not survive the crimes of social, cultural, and psychological violence during the voyage. At these seasoning farms, Africans endured a series of losses meant to strip them of their sense of self and self-worth. The first possession taken from the African was the most essential: They could no longer use their own names. Our names were tossed away as if they were not the sources of thousands of years of history and culture. Our ancestors felt the loss of their own ancestors because by losing one's name, one loses connection to a coherent society and culture. One becomes motherless, that is, without a nurturing community to give a sense of historical power. Furthermore, at the seasoning farm, young African women often lost their innocence and purity. In fact, the seasoning farm was so profoundly evil that the whites overseeing the seasoning considered any knowledge of Africa to be negative and against the white slave owner (Asante, 2009a).

All Africans' knowledge of the past had to be eradicated. They were not permitted to speak of African kings and queens who achieved greatness in their lands. They were not allowed to speak of African universities at Timbuktu, Gao, and Jenne. Nothing could be said about African empires such as Ghana, Mali, and Songhay. The slave makers felt that it was necessary to "break" their sense of pride, independence, confidence, and security. Slave makers' primary task was to sever bonds between enslaved Africans and those still on the continent. They were skilled at brutality but ignorant about culture and history and therefore had nothing but their own stereotyped opinions about Africans, ideas that had been developed by the preachers, priests, and philosophers of European culture. As far as these slave makers knew, Africans were heathens and did not have rights that had to be respected by any white person.

Once settled in the Americas on farms, the Africans who would become field Negroes were assigned to the master's most intense forms of labor, which required toiling in the sugar cane or cotton fields. In the words popularized by Malcolm X, they became known as field Negroes.

Africans in South America, North America, and the Caribbean went through similar processes. In some places, such as Colombia, Peru, and Brazil, Africans were forced to work in gold and copper mines. These, too, were the field Negroes or, as they were called, the mine Negroes, who were distinct from those who worked in the house of the slave owner. Although sugar cane and cotton were the two largest labor-intensive crops in the Americas, because slave owners also used Africans for nontechnical work around the plantations, the house Negro was able to gain specialized knowledge of white culture, which he or she could use to support the field Negroes if the house Negro was sufficiently conscious. This is what happened in the case of Toussaint L'Ouverture in Haiti, who, although not really a house Negro, was a stable hand and chauffeur. Nonetheless, he was able to organize an army of field Negroes to drive the French out of Haiti.

### African Masses

All Africans entering the Americas on slave ships were oppressed, but some were more seriously curtailed, constrained, restrained, and abused by the white population in a society where any white man could act as a master. If a slave holder considered an African to be assertive, angry, or confident, he aimed to break him or her down to prevent other blacks from emulating that behavior. Slave holders selected these spirited Africans to do the harshest work and receive the most brutal treatment. They were the laborers in the cities and field workers on the plantations. The white community justified their treatment of Africans by suggesting irrationally that Africans were inferior in intelligence to whites and immoral by nature. In southern folklore, every white slave owner recognized that such blacks, as field Negroes, were a potential force not to be ignored. Danger always lurked when Africans were unafraid of death and assertive enough to stand up for their rights (Gatewood, 1990).

## *The Skin Color Phenomenon*

Around the time of the American Revolution, over 150 years after the first Africans arrived in Jamestown, a mulatto population had developed, one that was large enough to be noticed by both the African and European groups (Reuter, 1969). Nevertheless, the American white culture considered mulattoes, who were essentially the products of white men having sex with black women, as black, not white. Mulattoes followed the classification of their mothers and not their white fathers. This policy position in the United States was meant to protect the idea of a white racial purity. This also meant that the African population became increasingly diverse and multicolored. Yet even among blacks, skin color often provided a formidable boundary, with some wrapping themselves in their pure African origins and others proving themselves to be more aggressively black than darker blacks. The abolitionist Frederick Douglass said that he thanked God that he was a man, but Charles Lenox Remond and Martin Delany, also aboltionists, thanked God that they were black men. There were also lighter-complexioned blacks who saw their white ancestry as proof that they were of a higher class than those Africans who were purely black. Consequently, suspicion of the Africans who were part-white arose in the African community because darker-skinned Africans thought that such a person would not be loyal to the black race. However, notwithstanding a few examples to the contrary, many of the ablest African American leaders were men and women with dual heritages. Citing examples ranging from Crispus Attucks, African and Native American, to Barack Obama, African and European, we find between these two black heroes hundreds of people of mixed race who have contributed greatly to the African American struggle. Therefore, as far as the black community is concerned, skin color does not carry significant weight in the struggle against oppression. Nevertheless, among whites, especially during the enslavement, some white slave masters used their mixed race children to betray the interests of their mothers. This was the source of color suspicion among blacks that was prevalent in the nineteenth century. Yet in the twentieth century, Booker T. Washington, W. E. B. Du Bois , and others proved that white paternity was not enough to deny blackness. During the mid-twentieth century, Adam Clayton Powell, Congressman from New York, and Walter White, Executive Secretary of the NAACP, would declare themselves to be black even though they were occasionally mistaken for white men. Hence, blackness was not simply a color but a state of mind. This also means that some of the darkest people can possess some of the most reactive and conservative views concerning the African American community. Thus, there were enslaved Africans who, although black in skin color, supported the interests of the white masters.

## How Racial Hierarchy Created Color Chaos

By the middle of the nineteenth century, northern whites felt themselves above the racial issues of southern planters. And because slavery existed in only some of the northern states because they did not have a large agrarian economy, they did not have the same fear of field Negroes as the Southerners. Nonetheless, whites in the North maintained a political color caste system no less oppressive than the Southern version because of what it symbolized (Gatewood, 1990). It encouraged the belief in mixed race superiority and the association of light skin with the ideal of beauty and goodness. Many darker-complexioned blacks criticized the idea that mixed race individuals should lead the fight against discrimination; in fact, they questioned the right of Booker T. Washington to speak for the black masses. These critics maintained that the mixed-blood blacks like Washington and Du Bois neither lived among them nor associated with them and, thus, could not convey their pain and suffering. Despite such resentment, many of the same dark-skinned blacks aspired to gain admission to the more exclusive mixed-blood societies. Furthermore, the records of Washington or Du Bois demonstrate nothing but complete identification with the plight of their black brothers and sisters. Although they disagreed with each other about tactics, they never wavered in their committed support for uplifting the black race because they saw themselves as a part of that community.

The slave system created a hierarchy of colors in which the lighter the skin of the African, the closer to the white race he was, and the higher the status of that person in the eyes of whites (Reuter, 1969). This meant that the light-skinned person could claim the myths of superiority, intelligence, and civilization—all baggage accompanying whiteness. Blacks who knew no better because of ignorance about their own history accepted these myths. Whites encouraged them, pointing out, when it was politically useful, that the most intelligent blacks were the lighter-complexioned ones. Setting up these distinctions led to the chaos that eventually produced poor consciousness among contemporary black conservatives. Regardless of their complexion, these black conservatives are the political descendants of those blacks who believed that they were given something special that set them apart from the masses, such as education at an Ivy League School, wealth, an association with elite white men, or hair texture or skin complexion. In fact, it did not have to be any one of these qualities in particular, but it is important to note that the individuals who were given the chances, the opportunities to advance both during and after the enslavement, were often the children of slave owners. These children of white slave owners were most prominent during the post–Civil War period as leaders, teachers, preachers, and legislators.

The presence of a significant number of mixed-race individuals brought up a number of questions for both whites and blacks regarding their status and role within the African community. Although data were collected by the National Census Bureau about mixed-race individuals during the nineteenth century, the existence of mixed-race blacks complicated record keepers' ability to accurately document population figures. Historians and social scientists generally believe that many blacks were counted as whites, although in the wider African American community, they would have been seen as blacks. According to relevant accounts, for example, it would have been difficult to determine who among the Louisiana state legislature were classified as "colored." Prior to the Civil War, there existed a large, free, colored population in New Orleans who were not necessarily light skinned or of mixed race. Free colored populations in the nineteenth century could be dark-skinned blacks. These blacks who had been free prior to the end of slavery were expected to provide political leadership during the post-war period.

During Reconstruction, many mixed-race persons held political office where their superior training and education could be put to use to service the African community. In Louisiana, light-skinned African leaders of the black community rose to positions of power after having acquired some measure of wealth as descendants of the slave-owning class. During this time, however, many able black leaders emerged to lead the African people in Louisiana. Some were local, whereas others traveled from out of state. Astonishingly, three leaders even reached the office of lieutenant governor: Oscar J. Dunn (1868–1871), Pinckney B. S. Pinchback (1871–1872), and C. C. Antoine (1872–1876). Additionally, there were African state officers, including P. G. Deslonde, secretary of state; Antoine Dubuclet, state treasurer; and W. G. Brown, superintendent of public education. What is even more amazing is that J. Willis Menard of New Orleans held the distinction of being the first African man certified as having been elected to the U.S. House of Representatives. However, uncomfortable with a black man serving in this post, Menard's white opponent challenged the election, and as a result, the House refused to seat him. Not to be discouraged, blacks then elected Charles E. Nash to the House of Representatives in 1874, who was to be the only Louisiana African American who officially sat as a member of Congress during Reconstruction.

One of these Africans who particularly distinguished himself during the Reconstruction was Oscar Dunn. Having been born into slavery, he managed to run away as a young man and gain his freedom, becoming a skilled plasterer and a violin teacher. Dunn was a unique individual who did not lack of courage and audacity when he disagreed with the Governor of the State, Henry C. Warmoth, and threatened to lead a Republican revolt against his government. As the first African official elected to a prestigious administrative post in any state of the Union, Dunn had exceptional intelligence, courage, and integrity. He was said to be incorruptible even by whites, who at the time thought most blacks lacked moral scruples. Oscar Dunn died suddenly in 1871.

## The Georgia Case

Several states, in addition to Louisiana, elected blacks during the Reconstruction. In Georgia, because blacks did not have the same power of numbers as in Louisiana, they won fewer legislative and political offices than blacks in Louisiana. Despite less numerical power, 3 blacks were elected to the state senate and 29 more to the lower house. In 1868, adopting a new constitution, whites, determined to compromise black participation in democracy, limited the meaning of democracy. According to that constitution, the law gave blacks the right to vote but not the right to hold public office. Blacks were then immediately removed from office, but after Congress intervened with military rule, these black leaders were reinstated.

Despite these disadvantages and setbacks, Georgia did contribute one of the most brilliant and militant leaders of the masses of blacks in the political process. Henry McNeal Turner was one of the best thinkers of his day. As a minister of the African Methodist Episcopal Church, Turner was beholden to no one but his black constituency. Furthermore, he had led an active life as a campaigner for black participation in the Civil War, during which he had been stationed in Washington, D.C. Specifically, he fought for the use of African troops, arguing astutely that the North would not be victorious without them. He joined the Union Army and soon became the first African chaplain commissioned by President Abraham Lincoln. He then moved to Georgia, keeping his post as chaplain, and there he joined the Freedmen's Bureau. Sometime later, he began educating ex-enslaved Africans, inspiring them to become politically active. Turner helped establish the Republican Party (later known as the party of Lincoln) in Georgia, and he later became a member of the Constitutional Convention. However, he did not get along well with white politicians in the legislature, who he saw as betraying the interests of the black masses. Turner asked Africans to neither trust whites nor fight for a nation that did not recognize their rights. He remained active in politics and religion, and after Reconstruction, he became a bishop in the African Methodist Episcopal Church. In this leadership role, Turner became known for advocating a back-to-Africa movement in the 1890s.

In Alabama, the proportion of blacks to whites was similar to that of Georgia during the Reconstruction. Although blacks constituted in excess of 90 percent of the Republican Party, they did not hold political offices proportionate to their presence in the party. Whites in Alabama had always held an intense prejudice against blacks, but after the South lost the Civil War, whites developed an increasingly intense hatred for blacks. Because of this animosity coupled with a lack of black political sophistication, developing outstanding black leadership proved to be quite challenging. In fact, during the Constitutional Convention of 1867, there were only 18 black delegates among a total of 90. When the first legislature after the Civil War convened, there were 26 blacks in a legislature composed of 84 members. There is no evidence that any blacks were elected to state office in Alabama during Reconstruction, although three blacks, including the influential James T. Rapier, did serve in the U.S. Congress.

Rapier fit the traditional image of a mixed-race leader. From Florence, Alabama, he was the son of a white planter and an enslaved African woman who was later freed by the slave-holding father of her child. After being educated by private tutors at the Scottish University of Glasgow and Montreal College in Canada, Rapier eventually became an accomplished scholar and skilled planter. He later sat as a member of the Constitutional Convention and was a member of the committee that authored Alabama's first Republican platform. He also ran as the Republican candidate for secretary of state office in 1870. Then in 1872 he was elected to Congress, where he became one of the most effective advocates of Charles Sumner's Civil Rights Bill.

In Florida, the state's position in the Confederacy and the proportion of blacks to whites set them slightly apart from the other southern states. Florida joined the Confederacy later than the other southern states. Furthermore, the population was much less dense than that in northern states, and whites outnumbered blacks by no more than 5,000 people. Politically, however, blacks still struggled for appropriate representation as they did elsewhere. At the state's Constitutional Convention in 1868, of the 45 delegates in attendance, 18 were black, and the state's initial legislature included 19 blacks out of a total of 76. Although several of Florida's African leaders were very talented politicians, whites made sure their numbers in office remained limited. However, an African man, Josiah T. Walls, did occupy Florida's lone seat in the U.S. House of Representatives.

Walls was a Civil War hero who, as a sergeant in the Union army, had moved to Florida and later settled there and became a successful planter. He was elected to Congress in 1870 after serving in the state's Constitutional Convention and the state legislature. After redistricting, Florida then gained two seats in the House, which led to Walls being reelected in 1872 and 1874. As was the case in other Southern states, angry, Confederate-sympathizing whites challenged the 1870 and 1874 elections, and Walls was then unseated after serving the major portion of his term. It is also worth noting here that according to historical accounts, Walls was generally a capable politician who served all of his constituencies regardless of their racial heritage.

Although today it is well known that blacks served at the national level during the Reconstruction, what is less known is that far more blacks were active at the state level. In fact, in Florida's state politics, one of the most able luminaries was an African man named Jonathan Gibbs. Gibbs was born in Philadelphia and had graduated from Dartmouth College, Princeton Theological Seminary, and later became a Presbyterian minister. Like other northerners, both black and white, he went south to help rehabilitate the African community. Gibbs initially decided to engage in missionary work with the newly freed enslaved Africans. However, not satisfied with this role, he realized he could better serve blacks in a secular position, so he served at Florida's Constitutional Convention of 1868, where he was most likely the best formally educated person there. Then, he worked as a cabinet member for Governor Harrison Reed. The governor soon realized that Gibbs's integrity was indisputable, and because of this, he appointed Gibbs as secretary of state. He was later appointed superintendent of public instruction in 1873 and then died suddenly in 1874 in Tallahassee.

In Virginia, where blacks first landed on American shores and where the proportion of blacks was about equal to that of Georgia and Alabama, blacks did not exercise the same political influence. In other states, including North Carolina, Arkansas, and Texas, the proportion of blacks to whites was even smaller. Virginia's African leadership was as capable as, and in some instances superior to, that of whites. However, whites' customary beliefs about blacks' inferiority and their ongoing anger over losing the war created animosities toward the black politicians that were so great that many of the noblest blacks never gained the authority that their counterparts had in other states. In fact, because the city of Richmond, Virginia, had been the Confederate capital and Virginia had been one of the leading states of the Confederacy, white sentiment against black participation in government ran high.

Historians have documented numerous accounts of African American leadership during the Reconstruction. Nevertheless, aside from the works of John R. Lynch, who published his memoirs, few authentic documents such as personal papers now exist because most were destroyed in the subsequent conservative reaction to black participation during its nadir after 1877. Consequently, historians only have access to accounts written by whites from that time, who often documented their own racially biased perspectives on black politicians. Needless to say, such documentation is extremely tainted by prejudice. These white writers tended to categorize all African politicians stereotypically. They took no account of individuality or the particular backgrounds or personalities of blacks—not even when those blacks were highly educated, as in the case of Jonathan Gibbs. Thus, the scarcity of documentation and the bias of what was left for record make it extremely difficult, if not impossible, to understand the true nature of African conservative leadership during those times. Fortunately, however, enough information exists in order to dispel some of the whites' bias toward and stereotypes of the black masses.

We can create a composite portrait of the black reconstructionist by examining the records we have. The group would have consisted of African carpetbaggers, ex-enslaved Africans, and freeborn blacks. Some were the sons of former slaveholders, but most were Africans recently freed from the plantations. Thus, in education and class, the individuals within this group varied significantly.

African American leaders during this period were notable for their diversity. Whereas some had been freeborn—Congressmen Revels, Walls, Ransier, Elliott, Cain, and Rapier—an account of the 16 African Congressmen in 1870 suggests that 10 had been previously enslaved. Of the 74 African delegates at South Carolina's Constitutional Convention, 38 had been enslaved Africans. Of those blacks elected to local positions, the number of former enslaved Africans was considerable. Although a large number were probably illiterate—as had been many whites who had served in the state legislatures—they were exceptionally intelligent and frequently educated themselves while serving in the legislature. Some were successful enough to operate profitable businesses, acquire a skilled trade, and, on occasion, practice law. As one commentator of the time stated, "The one thing that most native Negro leaders were not was fresh from the cotton fields" (Reuter, 1969, p. 46). The fact that so many of these legislators could have gone unnoticed in the cotton field dispelled any notions anyone could have of a mixed-race hypothesis about black leadership (Reuter, 1969). But whether light skinned or dark, freeborn or enslaved, the origin of African politics was in the service of the black masses. There were no black conservatives as we know them today because no such politician would have had access to a constituency. Black conservatism is preeminently a function of whiteness, white-influenced blacks, and blacks' desire to serve the interests of whites.

## Inspirational Models

Prior to the existence of black politicians, Congress and other legal conduits rarely advocated the issues that the black masses considered urgent. Most black politicians were assertive in their work to promote the interests of the masses. They were inspired by stories of Nat Turner, Gabriel Prosser, and Denmark Vesey. Their political paternity was neither that of the white Southerner nor the white Northerner but rather the radical activists who sought to create a better world for the masses. Black politicians entered the chambers of the various state legislatures and the Congress of the United States heartened with the memories of Harriet Tubman, Frederick Douglass, and Nat Turner.

Nat Turner's record was quite straightforward. He was born on October 2, 1800, and he died by execution on November 11, 1831, in Jerusalem, Virginia (Baker, 2008). Although there is some discrepancy about his birth, his death is certain. Turner was not content with the plight of blacks and believed he had a duty to make a change. Thus, in 1831 he led a violent slave rebellion in Southampton County, Virginia, in which 61 members of slave-holding families were killed. When the rebellion ended and Turner was captured and executed, the white population unleashed a barbaric killing spree that saw more than 300 Africans killed. It goes without saying that these revenge killings brought about the deaths of many innocents by roving mobs of frenzied whites. An all-white jury and judge tried and convicted Turner on November 5. The whites sentenced him to death by hanging, but the whites also decided to skin him. As was frequently the case when whites lynched African men in the South, they also mutilated Turner's body and then confiscated various body parts for souvenirs.

## The Rise of an Alternate Politician

By the turn of the century, the African American community began to divide politically. Some African Americans believed that the black race should aim principally to imitate the white race. Although there were not many blacks who thought this way, their numbers grew when a number of blacks who saw rugged individualism, apart from the condition of the masses, as a worthy enough challenge. They knew that racism existed, but they felt that they could gain personal advantage in wealth and status by staying away from any frontal struggle with whites, believing that there was no point to it when they should instead seek to accumulate wealth. Those who would become black conservatives did not see Nat Turner or Harriet Tubman as ideals; instead, whereas these blacks believed in lifting the masses, the black conservatives believed that concentrating on individual success was essential. Yet the most influential black leaders have been those who, like Turner, objected to the oppression of African people and put themselves in harm's way to fight for what was just. Anna Julia Cooper, who graduated from the Sorbonne with a PhD when she was in her sixties, would exclaim, "when and where I enter, my people enter with me"—and this would become the motto of the black nationalists.

Booker T. Washington, the most powerful black man of the early twentieth century, helped to bring into existence a class of African American leaders who might be called accommodationists. This class was strongly influenced by the ideology that blacks should seek to make themselves useful to whites. In his speech at the Atlanta Exposition in 1895, Washington laid out his philosophy that blacks and whites could be as separate as the fingers and as one as the hand. He believed that the African American's objective should not be social integration or political equality but rather the right to make money. This position would become the basis for the new black-conservative ideal of seeking individual achievement at the expense of collective uplift. We do not aim to dismiss the complexity of Washington's project, but we do suggest that it was his ideological position that helped to disseminate the seeds of black conservatism. There was a clear line leading from the house Negro type of thinking to the Washingtonian position.

When Marcus Garvey came to America from Jamaica in 1916, he was too late to meet Booker T. Washington, who died in 1915. Nevertheless, Garvey campaigned for the universal improvement of all black people and propagated the idea of "Africa for Africans." Considered the most important mass leader ever produced in the black race, Garvey was the lightning rod for an international organization of black people. He saw Washington supporting blacks' practice of self-determination; thus, he could accept that part of Washington's message. However, Garvey believed that the African person must be equal to any other person. Although there were some blacks who disputed Garvey's views, nearly 10 million people signed up as members of the Universal Negro Improvement Association and also the African Communities League, making his movement the most comprehensive unification of Africans in history.

## The Politics and the Skin Color Question

During the twentieth century, blackness retained a negative association. When the century opened, blacks were fighting for equal rights and the Ku Klux Klan was campaigning in the South as well as northern states such as Indiana and Pennsylvania to prevent blacks from exercising their rights, using violence against Africans to do so. Of course, the vast majority of Africans at the turn of the century were dark skinned, and the persecution of Africans was almost synonymous with the persecution of black-skinned people. This was not universally true, however, as many of the early fighters for justice were the descendants of the children of slaveholders. Because American society had declared that a person was black or Negro by virtue of having "one drop" of African blood, the lighter-complexioned Africans embraced their blackness, becoming as adamant as darker-skinned blacks against racism. Although it is true that some who were ideologically connected to the house Negro syndrome participated in a color stratification that defined the social structure in cities like New Orleans, Atlanta, and Washington, most lighter-complexioned blacks were firmly committed to the same principles as darker blacks. There were, after all, darker-complexioned blacks who were clearly house Negroes or aspired to be house Negroes. Furthermore, the type called Uncle Tom almost always referred to a darker-complexioned black who was willing to side with whites against the interests of equality and justice. In this regard, the question of color is far more complicated in American society than it seems at first sight. Certainly, the color line was not as clear and sharp as it was in South Africa, where all people who were of mixed race under the apartheid regime were classified as coloreds; nor was this line as contorted as in Brazil, where there were over 30 different color classifications of African-descended peoples.

Even blacks themselves instituted challenges that measured skin color gradations among other blacks. Some darker-skinned African Americans registered complaints against social organizations, especially the late nineteenth- and early twentieth-century Greek societies, stating that, some black sororities and fraternities had established color tests. For instance, if a person were darker than a brown paper bag, then he or she would not be invited to join the organization. Various social events, such as school dances, also required the "brown-paper-bag test" as a condition of admission. Spike Lee's film *School Daze* explored this form of colorism, and Robert E. Washington claimed that among fraternities and sororities darker-complexioned blacks were assessed a fee before they could be admitted, whereas lighter-skinned blacks were admitted free of charge (1990). Thus, white racial hierarchy, in which one was measured by their proximity to being white, had even permeated the social structure of the black community. Some of those bringing about these rules clearly followed the tradition of the house Negro; they held negative opinions about blackness, feared the contamination that would come with identification with dark skin, and wanted to demonstrate their superiority based on color. Having effectively imposed the structure inherited from white society on their own social situation, many of the ideological descendants of the house Negroes began to fear the inevitable rise of the black masses. Much like the whites who knew deep in their hearts that one day blacks would gain freedom, the descendants of the house Negroes knew that the majority of blacks would not be denied total freedom forever.

## Color and Identity in the Sixties

The Black Power Movement's motto "Black is Beautiful" changed everything in the black community, and this slogan was also on its way to changing America. Stating this meant that even those blacks who had made progress for the African American community by working for civil rights and marching against segregation had to dig deeper and find more blackness. On the black college campus and in black public arenas, the movement heralded as desirable the kinky hair, broad features, and dark skin shared by the majority of blacks. In contrast to the practices prior, organizations now rushed to find dark-skinned students to join fraternities and sororities because blackness was the new "in thing." Preachers wore their hair in the Afro style, women sought to outdo each other in how black they could look, and smooth black skin became the coin of the era.

Thus, the 1960s saw a rejuvenated interest in blackness as a physical characteristic. Playwrights, poets, and novelists rediscovered the Harlem

Renaissance authors who had celebrated blackness. As a result, Zora Neale Hurston, Langston Hughes, and Paul Laurence Dunbar were resurrected once more to perform their identity miracles where black skin took the position of moral authority in a nation that used skin color as a mark of degradation. Embracing all historical figures who worked in the interests of African Americans, from Martin Delany to Anna Julia Cooper, the children of the sixties established a common commitment to collective uplift as the mark of the authentic leader (Asante, 2009b). This was a rejection of all house Negroes. Perhaps the most noted leader other than Martin Luther King, Jr., was Malcolm X. Like an increasing number of African Americans whose ancestors had mixed with others and whose ancestry may have reached to white paternity—a pattern found in at least 35 percent of all African Americans—Malcolm X had white ancestry. Regardless, Malcolm X became the greatest icon of the black masses since the rise of Marcus Garvey in the earlier part of the century.

Born Malcolm Little on May 19, 1925, in the city of Omaha, Nebraska, his parents were Louise Norton Little, a homemaker who spent her time tending to Malcolm and his seven sisters and brothers. His father, Earl Little, was a proud African American and Baptist lay speaker who was not ashamed of his African features nor was he shy about his politics. Earl moved the family to Lansing, Michigan, where he became a Garveyite and preached that black people were equal to any other people and that Africa was the natural homeland for Africans. However, Earl won little favor from the Lansing, Michigan, white community. He was not a violent man but, like Garvey, was proud, determined, assertive, and very spiritual. His moral and spiritual conviction facilitated his political activism, which brought numerous death threats from the white supremacist groups, thus forcing the family to move within Lansing twice before Malcolm was four years old; however, their attempts to escape violence were unsuccessful. In 1929, at the beginning of the Great Depression, white racists burned the Littles' home to the ground. Shortly thereafter, whites murdered Malcolm's father, mutilating his body and leaving it on the trolley tracks. The white Lansing community cooperated with police to make sure that the arson of the Little home and Earl's murder would be determined as accidents. As the stress became too much for Malcolm's mother to endure, she suffered a nervous breakdown and was thereafter institutionalized. The state of Michigan assumed custody of Malcolm and his siblings by assigning them to local foster care or orphanages.

Academically, Malcolm was the smartest in his class of mostly white students. He graduated as the top student in his high school classes and aspired to become a lawyer, despite the murder of his father and institutionalization of his mother. Unfortunately, the school system did not support Malcolm's vision of his own worth and possibilities. Even though talented and bright, he could not overcome racist counseling white school officials had given. For instance, Malcolm's teacher confided to him that his desire to become a lawyer was "no realistic goal for a nigger" (Haley, 1996, p. 29). With his enthusiasm for higher educational goals extinguished, he dropped out of school and moved to Boston to live with a relative. After working a few odd jobs to support himself, Malcolm left Boston and moved to Harlem, New York, where he engaged in petty criminal activities. By 1942 he was earning a living dealing narcotics, pimping for prostitutes, and gambling illegally.

After his brief stay in New York, Malcolm moved back to Boston, where he and a friend were arrested and later convicted on a burglary charge in 1946 for which he received a sentence of seven years in prison. There, Malcolm took the time to return to education. He read extensively the books from the prison library, including the dictionary. When his brother Reginald visited, he exposed Malcolm to the religion of Islam. At first Malcolm resisted his brother's religious overtures but eventually gave in and converted. Although Malcolm's father and family had been Christians, Malcolm did not believe that Christianity could serve black people and argued that it was a group of Christians who had murdered his father and institutionalized his mother. In the Nation of Islam, Malcolm found the inspiration to devote his life to the welfare of the African people in general and of field Negroes in particular, with whom he identified.

After converting to Islam, Malcolm read the teachings of Elijah Muhammad, who was then the leader of the Nation of Islam. The Honorable Elijah Muhammad had been the victim of white racists because at the age of six he witnessed his father being lynched in a Georgia town. Similar to Nat Turner and Muhammad, the brutalities of white oppression had shaped Malcolm's political perspective. He identified with the field Negroes who had to seek complete freedom from racism on a daily basis. The Honorable Elijah Muhammad contended that African people experienced oppression in America because the white man was a devil. By the time Malcolm was released from prison in 1952, he had become an official member of the

Nation of Islam and assumed an "X" for a surname, meaning he was now an ex-slave who was free of the devil's domain. Furthermore, because African Americans could never come to know their original family names, the "X" was used as a fitting symbol for the unknown.

Malcolm X quickly rose within the ranks of the Nation of Islam. As one of its ministers he became a favorite of the Honorable Elijah Muhammad. He opened new mosques around the country, including in Detroit and Harlem. He communicated with the African people via the Nation's newspaper, *Muhammad Speaks,* as well as radio and television. Because Malcolm was able to reach the uneducated or undereducated blacks—the descendants of field Negroes—he convinced large numbers of similarly oppressed blacks to convert to Islam. Thus, historians credit Malcolm with increasing the Nation's following from as few as 1,000 in 1952 to 30,000 in 1963—a mere 11 years later.

As Malcolm's influence continued to grow, he began to attract the interest of mainstream white media. They considered him an African racist and were more interested in the shock value of his work rather than his attempts to rescue the African people from white oppression. Thus, in 1959 Mike Wallace of the popular *60 Minutes* news show featured Malcolm in a weeklong series of television specials titled "The Hate That Hate Produced." According to the series, Malcolm's hatred of white racism made him no different than the racist whites who had murdered his father. Ultimately, this series downplayed the legitimate political concerns that Malcolm had sought to rectify. In our judgment, Malcolm X's explanation of the house Negro and the field Negro as political concepts placed him at the vanguard of social analysis in the black community. The house Negro, as we have seen, was always willing to serve the white power system as a tool of black oppression (Haley, 1996). Conversely, the field Negro confronted all forms of injustice against the collective community of African people. Malcolm declared that he was a field Negro.

In 1963 Malcolm X delivered his "Message to the Grass Roots." By speaking of "grass roots," Malcolm underscored his interest in working to make the lives of the black masses better. It was in this speech that Malcolm made reference to the house Negro and field Negro (Malcolm X, 1963). His ability to construct such a powerful metaphor was unsurpassed by any spokesmen of his time. Those who came to hear him speak were so engrossed in his lectures that they were convinced that he was actually speaking to them personally. In a mix of scripture and historical fact, Malcolm conveyed the relevancy of field Negroes as fighters against evil, champions of the little people, and defenders of the rights and privileges of humanity, and he did so in language that blacks not only understood mentally but embraced emotionally:

> There were two kinds of enslaved Africans. There was the house Negro and the field Negro. The house Negroes—they lived in the house with master, they dressed pretty good, they ate good 'cause they ate his food—what he left. They lived in the attic or the basement, but still they lived near the master; and they loved their master more than the master loved himself. They would give their life to save the master's house quicker than the master would. The house Negro, if the master said, "We got a good house here," the house Negro would say, "Yeah, we got a good house here." Whenever the master said "we," he said "we." That's how you can tell a house Negro. (Malcolm X, 1963)

This trope became Malcolm's greatest rhetorical achievement in assessing the nature of black internal politics. The fact that his words ring true even in contemporary society demonstrates the extent of his rhetorical power. Indeed, he expanded the figure found in the historical record by suggesting other hypotheticals. For example, he stated,

> If the master's house caught on fire, the house Negro would fight harder to put the blaze out than the master would. If the master got sick, the house Negro would say, "What's the matter, boss, we sick?" We sick! He identified himself with his master more than his master identified with himself. And if you came to the house Negro and said, "Let's run away, let's escape, let's separate," the house Negro would look at you and say, "Man, you crazy. What you mean, separate? Where is there a better house than this? Where can I wear better clothes than this? Where can I eat better food than this?" That was that house Negro. In those days he was called a "house nigger." And that's what we call him today, because we've still got some house niggers running around here. (Malcolm X, 1963)

Politically, Malcolm X associated the modern-day house Negroes with the disinterested and uninvolved African American middle class who sought to distance themselves from the African community. They were the ones most likely to assign blame to blacks for poor social, economic, and political conditions while ignoring the role of racism and white oppression. Such blacks traveled in white circles where they might be the only blacks. They may have been the only black in their school, the only one on the board of directors, the only one as a full professor in the university, the only one in the neighborhood, and so forth. Politically, according to Malcolm X, such blacks harbored an even greater disdain for black people than many whites. These blacks knew that if it weren't for their white nationalist–oriented political perspectives, they might be counted among the illiterate, inferior, and despised Africans.

Unlike the house Negro, according to Malcolm, the field Negro wanted to separate himself from the white man. He wanted his own land where he could build his own community, manage his own school system, and otherwise take complete control of every aspect of black economic, social, and cultural development. Essentially, this was the concept of black nationalism, in which African Americans believed in their own ability to create institutions in their own interest and without white leadership. The key elements behind this view were self-determination, self-identity, and self-reliance in a community sense.

Malcolm articulated pride in being a field Negro. He recognized early on that for blacks to become motivated to political action, they must experience self-pride and self-worth. Malcolm, therefore, rejected being called "colored" or "Negro" as derogatory terms invented by the white system of enslavement and racial hierarchy. Africans had to relinquish the names that whites had given them and adopt names that honored their ancestors. Through this practice, Malcolm taught pride and identity. The monumental civilizations of Africa in Kemet, Nubia, Axum, Ghana, Mali, and Songhay were to be celebrated and respected.

Black people can control their political and cultural destiny by assuming responsibility for African identity and history. Nevertheless, one had to be vigilant because the institutions that sought to prevent black pride and achievement during the enslavement had transformed into some of the most visible institutions prohibiting and combating blacks in the twentieth and twenty-first centuries. Police brutality and harassment obstruct, frustrate, and badger black people, especially black men. During slavery, field Negroes were punished with whippings, torture, and injuries; now black men are arrested, with police officers citing resisting arrest, when black men questioned the behavior of those police officers; employers refuse to promote blacks who raise questions about racism in employment; administrators attempt to discipline blacks who point out the double standards used when whites seek to appoint blacks to positions and when they seek to appoint whites to similar positions; and other racist actions continue pervasively. When an administrator demands less from blacks, it is a form of racism because it indulges the idea that blacks are inferior.

The black masses are still resigned to the poorest housing stock, the worst medical care, and the lowest paying jobs. Despite the progress that has been made in the political arena, the great majority of blacks have not seen their conditions change dramatically. In fact, according to the Bureau of Labor Statistics for May 2010, unemployment among blacks was 15.5 percent, as compared to around 8.8 percent for whites.

\* \* \*

None of Malcolm's contemporaries—particularly Martin Luther King, A. Philip Randolph, Roy Wilkins, or John Lewis—used the plantation metaphor as well as he did. In addition to field Negroes and house Negroes, Malcolm frequently referenced the Uncle Tom, which was any African who assisted the white slave masters oppress other blacks. In the late nineteenth century, this was the most hated name that a black could be called, and Malcolm did not hesitate to reference what he called "twentieth-century Uncle Toms"—those who helped maintain control of the African community by keeping it passive and nonviolent. This was also a not-so-subtle remark directed at Martin Luther King, Jr. Although King did not refer to field Negroes personally, he did, in fact, advocate and articulate their issues. Similar to Malcolm, King was an African icon whose political activism changed the quality of life for the masses of the African community (Kirk, 2007).

No other historical event in America has impacted the political struggles of African folk as deeply as the enslavement. Harold Cruse understood the fact that African American intellectuals have remained victims of the enslavement, imprisoned by whites' hatred of blacks made apparent through a rabid white racism that holds black and whites both in psychological bondage. Thus, we are still experiencing the aftermath of the enslavement in various ways, one of the most dramatic of which is the development of the black conservatives. They are caught between the narrative of reality and the myth of individualism and have largely decided to choose the myth of individuality over the realities of racism.

## *Toward a New Direction*

The 1960s, the decade when Malcolm X termed African people in the United States African Americans, marked a critical turning point in American politics and perhaps Western civilization. Voting and other rights for African people had been secured in 1964, once again giving African Americans the political power they had once enjoyed during the post–Civil War Reconstruction era. Political leaders emerged from every sector of the African community to be elected as mayors, city councilmen, attorney generals, and members of Congress. For the first time in American history, African folk became recognized de jure as equal to white Americans in the eyes of the democratic union. Blacks no longer represented only African constituencies. Particularly, young urban whites—commonly known as yuppies—who did subscribe to the tenants of white supremacy, began to make decisions about who they voted for less on the basis of race and more on qualifications. Astonishingly, in 2008 this change of the white political mindset resulted in the election of America's first black, that is, African American, president in its history. President Barack Obama introduced a newer, more inclusive brand of politics that, similar to his constituency, depended less on race and more on the ideals of freedom, justice, and equality (Obama, 2006). However, despite the fact that younger as well as other whites, Latinos, Asians, and Native Americans supported the first African American for president, the presence of house Negroes who opposed racial progress persisted. Aligned with hard-line racist whites, particularly from the Conservative South, these black conservatives actively participated in campaigns to oppose the election of Obama. They could no longer be identified by skin color or mixed-blood heritage, but they nonetheless fervently disdained the masses of the African community, which now included all members of the African population.

Similar to antebellum house Negroes, black conservatives frequently originate with those who believe that they are more refined than the masses.

As in the case of Supreme Court Justice Clarence Thomas, one's class origin or regional origin does not always dictate one's political philosophy, but rather it is one's understanding of American history and one's experiences as a human being. Thomas will be treated in a later section in the book, but for now we want to introduce him as a contemporary model descendant of the house Negro.

House Negroes today operate in style, opinion, vision, and expertise according to the cultural norms of the conservative white community. Many make their living with white "think tanks" advocating political policies that counter the welfare of the African community (Toppo, 2005). They are sometimes a talented but misdirected lot, whose political aspirations ignore racism and the enslavement, seeing them as irrelevant to the life opportunities and state of African Americans today. If not in bloodline, then certainly by class orientations, behavior, philosophy, and demeanor, these black conservatives descend socially and politically from the antebellum house Negroes. They are usually members of conservative white religious denominations, that is, white churches dominated by white leadership. They are rarely atheists, Africanists, or Muslims; philosophically, they follow the European tradition.

# CHAPTER THREE

# *House Negroes and the Crisis of Identity*

In most areas of the antebellum South, the enslaved African woke up every morning to the world of the plantation. Everything he knew was centered on the master's plantation. If useful new information came to the plantation, it usually came when Africans from other plantations were sold to one's master. Although the system was tight and fixed, day in and day out, an enslaved African could often use his or her imagination to weave narratives and visions of victories that they had never seen nor heard of—the kinds of stories that the plantation owners tried to ensure that their own enslaved people never heard about: uprisings, killings, or plots to destroy crops (Asante, 2001; Bennett, 2007; Stampp, 1989). Those who labored under a master's subjugation might experience their entire lives having never ventured more than a mile or two from the plantation. In the event that an enslaved African was required to travel, he did so only at the master's discretion and with his permission. To do otherwise was considered an attempt to escape. By word of mouth, every African heard stories about those who had tried and failed to escape the plantation, making any thoughts of doing so less appealing. The plantation psychology was reiterated repeatedly to Africans: If they wanted to escape, they could not do so successfully because there would be no place to go to for survival assistance. This was intended to make the African feel helpless and hopeless. Nevertheless, by the 1840s escapes had become so common in the American South that plantation leaders had decided that the old system was unsustainable. However, it is also true that, as a result of the stories told about the difficulties of escaping, there were some enslaved Africans who sought to endure their circumstances until they could be assured that leaving the plantation would not render their lives more brutal than what they already suffered. This was usually the course of the house Negroes.

Although the majority of enslaved Africans worked the fields and took to the tasks of hard labor, even those who worked in the master's house were never far from the constant dangers of bondage. The slave master was all-powerful, so that any African man, woman, or child was at the mercy of their master, who might abuse them at any moment. Slave women in particular were exposed to a particularly perverse abuse, having been raped repeatedly by the slave master, to the extent that this practice became an American institution (Bennett, 2007). The fervent sermons of white preachers who espoused the rhetoric of Christianity rarely condemned such rampant violation of black men and women. The slave master, his sons, his overseers, and any white male associated with his plantation frequently took sexual advantage of African women who were powerless to defend themselves. Whether they were mothers, daughters, children, or single heads of household, any day might find an unsuspecting African female the focus of white male lust. In fact, few among slave women had passed through puberty without having been raped or otherwise sexually molested by plantation-propertied white males (Asante, 2009a).

Because white males routinely raped enslaved women, a new racial class of enslaved African eventually emerged, as shown in the DNA analyses of Henry Louis Gates, Jr., and the African Ancestry organization. Their bloodline and, thus, racial heritage was a composite of the master and his enslaved rape victims. No wonder Gates, who is half Irish, claims that nearly half of all African Americans have white ancestry. Gerald Norde's powerful 2008 book, *Peculiar Affinity: The World the Slave Owners and their Female Slaves Made*, demonstrates the extent of the mixing of DNA. Norde estimated that the slave owners impregnated enough young African women to produce between 5 and 7 million children, who, over time, were sold as "Negroes" on the chattel commodity market. During slavery, often the physical features of the mixed-race slaves were distinguishable from both the master and his enslaved Africans, but sometimes they were not. Some of these individuals might be characterized by blond hair and eyes as blue as the master's. Others might appear African in features, including dark skin, with white characteristics such as keen noses and straight hair. As the master's offspring, these mixed-race slaves descended from field Negroes were often accorded a different manner of treatment, though they were nevertheless enslaved Africans (Bennett, 2007). Most were assigned by the master to less laborious jobs in the master's house, where they were shielded from the intensely hot southern sun or spared the overseers' brutal lash. Those who curried particular favor from the master might acquire a measure of wealth—at least by the enslaved Africans' standards—be taught to read, or even receive an education at the master's expense. Living in the master's house as servants and kitchen help, they took the master's culture and norms as their own. Although they were still enslaved, they often saw their status as different socially, politically, and culturally from that of the usually darker-complexioned field Negroes (Haley, 1996). They could be expected to criticize the Africans who escaped or tried to escape from bondage. Furthermore, when the field Negroes attempted to strike for freedom, the house Negroes experienced more difficulty convincing their slave masters that even they could be trusted.

Many descendants of the house Negroes who were the offspring of the white master class became part of the African American elite at the end of the Civil War. Furthermore, their intimacy with the master class exacerbated an already formidable color-based political schism within the African community. In fact, the use of the term *colored* to describe black people after the Civil War was largely the result of social promotion by the African American elite. The vast majority of blacks never understood the concept "colored" in reference to themselves because they recognized their blackness and African origin. However, both terms, *black* and *colored,* came to carry negative connotations in the early twentieth century. Although "African" had been a part of the name of the African Methodist Episcopal Church (AME) in 1793, a hundred years later the word "colored" had replaced it in most titles related to black people.

Whites justified their political oppression of African people, slavery and segregation, with appeals to race. Despite the mixed-race bloodlines of house Negroes, eugenicists and especially Southern "scholars" proposed that race could be determined by a "rigid criteria" of biological heritage implied to some extent by appearance, such as the skin color of field Negroes versus house Negroes. Southern antebellum laws often referred to certain blacks as quadroon or octoroon because they had white paternity somewhere in their lineage. Quadroons (one-quarter African American but still darker skinned) and octoroons (one-eighth African American), who were considered exotic, were in particularly high demand by sexually exploitative master-class white males (Gatewood, 1990). They were called "fancy girls" and were auctioned at "quadroon balls" that were held regularly in New Orleans and Charleston. A respectable "gentleman" might buy one, and when he tired of her, six months or so later, he bought himself another. If he found one he liked, he might keep her for life. However, sometimes the use of the term *mixed race* sufficed. For political reasons, the legal establishment assumed that racial heritage could be proven in a court of law, but, in fact, this was not consistently possible if litigants were of mixed race. This was a significant issue for whites given that it could possibly have legal implications for wealth, status, and other quality-of-life assessments in America. As the mixed-race population grew, the need for a more discrete system of differentiation likewise increased.

As numerous race cases permeated the courts, other institutions such as the census experienced even greater difficulty prior to the end of the Civil War. Local communities utilized a less quantifiable but practical solution by applying personal knowledge in order to assess a black's status as either a "free house Negro" or a "bonded field Negro," which of course amounted to little more than personal preference or even racist opinion. Thus, the manner in which whites assessed blacks not only determined their racial heritage but also whether or not they were free to take part in the privileges and opportunities allowed ordinary white American citizens. Few systems of categorization could have been less objective and/or scientific than race. Accordingly, when the District of Columbia decided to abolish slavery in 1862, the owners of enslaved Africans were required to complete documentation of house Negroes and field Negroes as their prior property by describing skin color. This description included designating color by the following: "dark black, quite black, light black, dark brown, light brown, chestnut, dark chestnut, copper-colored, dark copper, light copper, yellow, dark yellow, bright yellow, pale yellow, very light, and nearly white" (Reuter, 1969). Such official terms of category make apparent the absurdity of a taxonomy based on skin color that had been created by white slave owners who were having sex with African women across the color spectrum. The hypocrisy of the situation was not only backward and blatant, but unredeemable, lingering as a legacy of the enslavement.

Although the slave masters' sexual liaisons with African women were responsible for the majority of mixed-race house Negroes, white women were not unknown to become pregnant by either field Negroes or house Negroes. However, these were treated in stark contrast to the white male–African female unions. Nonetheless, house Negroes on occasion were the offspring of African male and white female unions. Beginning in the 1840s, court disputes involving the offspring of such unions increased annually and placed considerable burden on legal personnel, who worked within the confines of the antebellum court system to sort out the problems. House Negroes, who were otherwise the biological offspring of the master class, whether male or female, jeopardized the "eugenic" association of blackness with slavery and whiteness with freedom, making biological origin the core issue of the race matter at the time. A particular complication involved enslaved blacks who, because of their mixed-race heritage, were light in skin color but, because their mothers were enslaved Africans, were left to a similar life of bondage. Other instances involved dark-skinned free blacks who were continually required to provide evidence to legal authorities of their free status. Some attempted to conceal their heritage by claiming descent from English, Spanish, Portuguese, or Native American ancestry.

Racial heritage was critical for determining not only freedom for house Negroes but their inheritance of wealth and property as well. Thus, two 1850 Georgia court cases made apparent the manner in which the race category could be challenged legally and in the social community (Reuter, 1969). Both cases involved the male offspring of a white mother. Both cases offered conflicting testimony from members of the local community as to whether the fathers had been dark-skinned field Negro men. Despite harsh taboos against such interracial sex between African men and white women, the community, however tacitly, tolerated its existence, a tolerance that the courts could not acknowledge officially in public documents. In resolving these cases, much of the conflicting testimony among members of the white community centered on the acknowledgment of interracial sex, with some people conceding its occurrence, whereas others, for traditional reasons, denied it. When wealth was involved, resolving the criteria for determining race became more critical, whereas it might otherwise have been considered less significant. This issue of wealth was one of the most potent factors inspiring house Negroes to distance themselves politically from the masses of the impoverished field Negro African community. To do otherwise might jeopardize the relatively privileged lifestyles most house Negroes had come to know. Thus, they felt rescued by their mixed-race blood, as many were the offspring not of some poor ignorant Irish overseer but, in fact, the progeny of the upper-class and, in some cases, even historical icons, such as Sally Hemings and the third president of the United States, Thomas Jefferson.

Even though raping African women could be expected in lesser men, scholars, including Barbara Chase-Riboud and William Cobbett, generally hold that Jefferson engaged for many years in sexual intercourse with a slave girl named Sally Hemings, who was 14 years old when it began (Reuter, 1969). This is perhaps the most famous and controversial case of a white antebellum elite "gentleman" keeping a black concubine. Although in this instance the white man was also an author of the Declaration of Independence and the third president of the United States, Jefferson's actions are not atypical but rather quite within the realm of the mores of the Southern whites at the time.

Scholars generally accept that in 1772 Thomas Jefferson married a widow named Martha (Wayles) Skelton, the daughter of John Wayles, a prosperous local plantation owner, Martha's father, a widower, kept a light-skinned house Negro slave named Betty Hemings as a concubine. Shortly after Jefferson and Martha's marriage, the concubine gave birth to a daughter, Sally, who, in the context of slave culture, became Martha's illegitimate half-sister. John Wayles died not long after Sally's birth, and Martha inherited 40,000 acres of land and 135 enslaved Africans, including Betty and Sally Hemings (Appleby, 2003; Burstein, 2005; Cunningham, 1988).

Jefferson's marriage to Martha was by all indications a happy one. She bore him six children, although only two survived to adulthood. However, she suffered from poor health and had frequent miscarriages, and she eventually died at the age of 33 after 10 years of marriage. At the time, Sally was 9 years old and serving as Martha's personal servant. Jefferson was extremely distraught over his wife's death and turned to public service to escape his depression. He spent two years as a delegate to the Continental Congress, and then, in 1784 he left for Europe, taking his two oldest children with him. After a year in London, he moved to Paris, where he served nearly four years as the U.S. minister to France.

While in Paris, Jefferson received more tragic news from home. His second youngest child had died. Grief stricken at losing yet another family member, he sent for his youngest daughter, Polly. An older slave, who was supposed to accompany Polly on the long journey to Europe, took ill, and Jefferson's household hurriedly decided to send Sally Hemings instead. Sally was then 14 years old and already showing the unmistakable signs of burgeoning womanhood.

Some historians believe that Jefferson began having intercourse with Hemings almost immediately after her arrival in Paris. His journal provides one possible indication of his growing obsession with her. Prior to her arrival in Paris, Jefferson used the word "mulatto" only once in 48 pages, but shortly after her appearance, "mulatto" appeared eight times in fewer than 25 pages. He described even the countryside of Holland as "mulatto"—a curious adjective for the highly literate Jefferson to employ about the landscape.

When Jefferson was preparing to return to America in 1789, Hemings announced to Jefferson that she was pregnant, presumably with his child. At that point, she was forced to decide whether to accompany Jefferson back to America or to stay abroad. She would be free as long as she lived in France, but if she returned to America she would return to slavery. Jefferson allegedly persuaded her by promising her material wealth and guaranteeing freedom for her unborn child.

Back in the States, around 1801, Jefferson was sworn in as the third president of the United States. Some believe that he and Hemings were still sexually involved, after more than 10 years since their return from Paris. She continued to live at Monticello, his Charlottesville estate in Virginia, the same state where some years later Nat Turner would lead a bloody uprising against slavery. Over the years, Hemings bore five more children. The question of whether Jefferson fathered any or all of them has become a source of national controversy. In an effort to sanitize his image, some biographic scholars have suggested that, in fact, the father of Sally Hemings's children was one of Jefferson's nephews, not Jefferson himself. However, the fact that in Jefferson's will, of all the enslaved Africans on his plantation, only Sally's children were allowed to go north to freedom contradicts this claim.

Many Western scholars have largely ignored the possibility that Thomas Jefferson may have engaged in sexual intercourse with a 14-year-old girl. Perhaps they found it hard to believe that the same person who wrote that "all men are created equal" not only owned enslaved Africans but actually sexually exploited at least one of them. Several decades passed after

Jefferson's death before any of the evidence of this alleged liaison with Hemings was examined, and by then much of it had been lost or destroyed.

In an attempt to resolve the Jefferson controversy, genetic scientists Foster, Jobling, Taylor, Donnelly, de Knijff, Mieremet, Zerjal, and Tyler-Smith compared Y-chromosomal DNA from male-line descendants of Field Jefferson, a paternal uncle of Thomas Jefferson, with those of male-line descendants of Thomas Woodson, Sally Hemings's first son, and Eston Hemings Jefferson, her last son. The molecular findings do not support the claim that Jefferson was Thomas Woodson's father, but they do provide evidence that Jefferson was the biological father of Eston Hemings Jefferson.

In 1802 the third president of the United States was first alleged to have fathered this illegitimate son of Sally Hemings. Hemings named the child Thomas, and most historians think he was born in 1790, shortly after Jefferson and Hemings returned from France. Members of the Woodson family today have long believed that Thomas Jefferson was the father of Thomas Woodson, whose family name comes from his later owner. The family's claim, however, has never been taken seriously by presidential scholars, historians, or society—no doubt largely because of what this claim would imply about the lack of morality at one of the highest levels of Western civilization.

Sally Hemings had at least four other children. Her last son, Eston (born in 1808), is said to have held a striking resemblance to Thomas Jefferson. As a result, he became a house Negro who "passed" for white as a way to distance himself from the despised lowly African community. He settled down in Madison, Wisconsin, and took the name Eston Hemings Jefferson. Although his descendants believe that Thomas Jefferson was Eston's father, so-called Jefferson scholars give more credence to the oral tradition of the descendants of Martha Jefferson Randolph, the president's legitimate daughter. She contends that Sally Hemings's later children, including Eston, were, in fact, the offspring of either Samuel or Peter Carr, sons of Jefferson's sister, which would explain their resemblance to the president. Science, however, has ultimately sided with the descendants of Sally Hemings.

Genetic scientists have determined that, apart from occasional mutations, most of the Y chromosome is passed, unchanged, from father to son. A DNA analysis of the Y chromosome can reveal whether or not individuals are likely to be male-line relatives. Those involved with the Jefferson study therefore analyzed DNA from the Y chromosomes of five male-line descendants of two sons of the president's paternal uncle, Field Jefferson; five male-line descendants of two sons of Thomas Woodson; one male-line descendant of Eston Hemings Jefferson; and three male-line descendants of three sons of John Carr, grandfather of Samuel and Peter Carr. No Y-chromosome data were available from male-line descendants of Thomas Jefferson because he had no known surviving sons.

Four of the five male-line descendants of Thomas Woodson were proven unrelated, although they were characteristically Caucasian in origin. The fifth Woodson descendant was linked genetically to Africans. Conversely, the descendant of Eston Hemings Jefferson was genetically linked to Field Jefferson. The genetic materials of two of the descendants of John Carr were identical; the third differed only slightly. The Carr genetic material differed substantially from those of the descendants of Field Jefferson.

In conclusion, Foster, et al. found that although Thomas Woodson was not Thomas Jefferson's son, Thomas Jefferson, rather than one of the Carr brothers, was the father of Eston Hemings Jefferson. As a result, serious scholars cannot doubt that Thomas Jefferson, one of the most esteemed figures in American history, fathered black children. In 1997 Dinitia Smith and Nicholas Wade of the *New York Times* noted that DNA tests performed on descendants of Thomas Jefferson's family and of his house slave Sally Hemings offer new evidence that the third president of the United States fathered at least one of her children. According to their report, Jefferson, when he was almost fifty years of age, had taken advantage of a 14-year-old female house slave he owned. These findings again confirm an oral tradition that has been handed down among Hemings's descendants for generations—that they are, in fact, also descendants of the third president of the United States (Reuter, 1969). Their association with the master class was not irrelevant to their sense of identity as contemporary Americans.

Most historians believe the number of African elite was quite small. However, in comparison to field Negroes, the African social elite who descended from house Negroes lived relatively lavish lifestyles. Similar to whites, they distinguished themselves from those who were the newcomers as "old family" elite. At various times and places, this social elite class of African people was known as the "colored aristocracy," the "African 400," the "upper tens," and "best society" (Reuter, 1969). Although not all of these people descended from the house Negroes, a great many of them were, nonetheless, related.

The African social elite often regarded themselves as privileged, and this determination was based on their values, norms, traditions, education, and other characteristics that reflected those of the white community. They were sure to make reference to the fact that the African community was not a monolith and then go on to state that although the masses of illiterate, lower-class blacks may be justly regarded as inferior, the elite among them were as civilized and poised as any white person. Poor whites felt offended by this attitude, referring to these blacks as "uppity," with the elite blacks referring to the whites as "PWT." The black masses recognized that the black elite seemed eager to improve themselves at the expense of the masses, which created tensions between the two groups. The masses' anger against the elite was just as intense as the anger against whites. Seeking to ride to individual freedom on the horse of hard work and entitlement, the social elite almost always disidentified with the plight of the masses.

African elite communities were evident in the shadows of Southern plantations, where just a few short years prior, many Africans had lived and worked as slaves. Although most whites in the South and elsewhere regarded the whole of African folk as inferior, some did acknowledge existing class distinctions. For instance, in 1877 a Southerner employed as a writer for the *Atlantic* magazine noted an elite class among African South Carolinians who practiced a rigid form of social ranking and discrimination (Baker, 2008). In daily life they took painstaking measures to see to it that no lowly, dark-skinned, farm-laboring black could enter their ranks either by marriage, social circumstances, or community affairs. On occasion, an African outsider, regardless of complexion, who managed to acquire unusual wealth or prestige, might be privileged to enter the ranks of the African elite; even then, however, within such ranks, they would be less than equal to established members.

Whatever the circumstances, a discriminating African elite existed throughout the American South in both small towns and large cities. Another white journalist reported that in the South, there were two factions of aristocratic African elite evolving: an aristocracy of culture and an aristocracy of wealth. However, regardless of which faction the African elite might aspire to, their status within the community was grounded in their official station in life; their church position; their amount of wealth, including money or real estate; their previous ownership; and the city where they were born. Additionally, when such criteria were satisfactory, the issue of skin color was still not irrelevant to overall importance (Baker, 2008).

A few years ago, Ronald Hall took note of the elaborate class distinctions young black adults made among themselves by listening to and observing their views on skin color. The author concluded that when it comes to issues of dating, sibling organizations, aesthetics, and social relationships, distinctions made on the basis of color are still quite active and alive in contemporary society.

During the 1960s, even in the smallest of southern towns, one could still find at least one elite family who descended from some white family or house Negro. Membership in such a clan required an African person to be born into the class, thereby assuming money, education, and a style of conduct that was expressive of one's history. The group sustained itself by selective marriage only with those who possessed similar qualities. When exceptions were made, education or some extraordinary accomplishment might suffice, but wealth alone would never prove satisfactory. Those lighter in skin color experienced greater leniency getting exceptions made, compared to those who were darker skinned or otherwise held striking resemblances to low socioeconomic-class blacks.

Given that the African elite were often the descendants of antebellum house Negroes, they were much less of a threat socially and politically to the white community. However, for the most part, the black elite supported white privilege as a function of the social order that gave them their status by virtue of skin color and opportunity. They became the first among blacks to be educated, gain professional employment, and, thus, become the first leaders of the African community. They resided in the best houses in the African community; traveled for northern vacations; and provided books, musical instruments, and education for their children at Hampton, Howard, Spelman, and Morehouse. It sometimes seemed that they feared the "Negro" more than they feared the whites because they felt that the descendants of the field Negroes could mess things up for them. They never wanted to be seen in the same category as the field Negroes. They feared reverting back to a slave status, and as a result, they placed great emphasis on acquiring an education. The educations they desired most were those that prepared their children to assume a professional occupation such as doctor, lawyer, or minister. Those who became doctors would be immune to failure, thus securing their status as members of the African elite. Being a professional, they could have contact with the black underclass without being stained by association. They perceived themselves as setting examples for lower-class blacks. They believed that they could help all blacks aspire to be professionals, members of society, fraternities, sororities, and church associations that would instill the best morals, ideals, cultural poise, and general self-improvement.

The black masses went along with their business—protesting and fighting racism and colorism—as if the elite did not exist. They were forced to join the movement for total freedom in the 1940s when A. Philip Randolph's Brotherhood of Sleeping Car Porters emerged as the largest, best organized group of black workers in the United States. Whereas many of the elite had ignored Marcus Garvey's earlier call to the black race to unite, they could not dismiss the significance of Randolph, the erudite, sharp-tongued rationalist. The black majority considered the elite to be too arrogant and far removed from the African community to make any kind of alliance between the two groups. Initially, common goals and objectives were virtually impossible, which made many elite blacks feel that they were unappreciated by the masses. It would not be until the 1950s and 1960s that the lighter-complexioned blacks would finally make the break with their social status past and join the ranks of the Civil Rights Movement. They had behind them the histories of Adam Clayton Powell, Andrew Young, Leon Sullivan, and other lighter-complexioned blacks who threw their political marbles into the ring with the rest of the black community. The triumph of common objectives in overcoming discrimination, segregation, and racism was a clear sign that color distinctions were becoming less of a factor in the lives of African Americans. When Angela Davis, Haki Madhubuti, Nikki Giovanni, and other young activists went to the frontlines of our conflict with injustice, they did not go as "colored" but rather as blacks who identified with the field Negro tradition. Just as whites who traveled to the South after the Civil War saw the black population at a missionary field, the black elite looked at the masses of blacks as their burden. Much blame was laid at the feet of poor blacks during the early twentieth century. Whatever evil plagued the nation was the result of the black presence. If there were hungry people, it was not because those who owned the companies refused to hire black workers; instead, it was because black people were considered lazy. In 1893, in the town of Knoxville, Tennessee, a member of the African aristocratic elite suggested that the potential of his class suffered as a consequence of the lack of morals and culture displayed by the masses of the underclass field Negroes. In an effort to remedy the problem, he suggested requiring even greater differentiations within the African community and an ever more rigid observance of these differentiations than had been practiced in the past. Accordingly, doing this would make it easier to separate out the immoral and dysfunctional elements so that they could no longer impose themselves on the race as a whole (Baker, 2008). Rather than understanding the entire context for Africans' social and economic breakdown—246 years of enslavement—elites sought to blame a group of blacks and then excise them from the community.

The rich class of both whites and blacks tends to operate in similar fashions. They both have their own patterns, acculturation styles, behaviors, and opinions. Both groups tend to hold the lowest elements of the white community with disdain. Thus, class trumps race. However, among whites, both rich and poor alike, blacks are seen as having little class differences.

Whites could usually live in any area of any town despite racial discrimination imposed on black housing. However, during the twentieth century, in some communities there were ordinances against whites living in black areas or blacks living in white areas. Indeed, segregation laws demanded that whites and blacks not live in the same houses. Even with an increase in mixed-race children, as during the last days of the enslavement, the social taboo of whites and blacks living in the same community was too strong to overcome in most cases. At least publicly, within the white community, the strict separation of the races enabled the public appearance of race separation. Life and social traditions, especially in the urban North, were different than those in the South. Slavery did not keep a foothold in the North and segregation was not overtly the custom there; furthermore, the predominance of urban life in the North served as a vehicle for interaction between the races in ways that were not possible in the South. Despite the fact that northern urban areas offered more opportunities for racial integration, the interaction between the African elite descendants of house Negroes and the underclass field Negroes remained difficult and separate. In the South, the descendents of house Negroes were more often referred to as aristocrats, whereas in the North, they were more often designated as the "upper tens."

Similar to their southern counterparts, the African aristocratic elite in the North in cities such as New York and Philadelphia emphasized family background, education, tradition, and respectability within the community. They included lawyers, doctors, salaried employees, business owners, and entertainers. As was customary, they sought to distance themselves from the masses of field Negroes whenever possible. The people most assertive about class were proud to be members of the older established African families. Being a member of an older African elite family meant that one's relatives had arrived in the North prior to the Civil War. Among the older upper tens in Boston were African families such as the Duprees, Haydens, Walkers, Baldwins, Allstons, Lattimores, and Ruffins (Hall, 1994). Some of the most outstanding members of this group, according to Gatewood (1990), were the descendants of Brazillia Lew, an African Bostonian said to have taken part in the American Revolution. Like other upper tens, the Lew family was not particularly wealthy, but their history participating in the Revolutionary War entitled them to membership in Boston's African upper tens. In 1952 eight generations of the Lew family played significant roles in the social and civic life of the Boston African community (Gatewood, 1990).

The upper tens, although quite discreet in membership, were not averse to fraternizing with black Southerners. They favored families such as the Grimkes, the Trotters, the Ridleys, and the Chappelles for their distinguished family backgrounds (Gatewood, 1990). The upper tens were known to be socially exclusive but did seek out and encourage associations with whites. These Northern upper ten descendants of house Negroes with few exceptions were always light skinned. They took offense to being referred to as Negroes. One such member of the upper tens reported to a white investigator writing about the African community:

> When you write of the Negroes of Boston tell about us who are neither Negroes nor whites, but an ambiguous something-between a people not yet known or named. While our sympathies tend to unite us with the Negroes and their destiny, all our aspirations lead us toward white. (Gatewood, 1990, p. 78)

Thus, segregation in the North was less practiced than it was in the South. Consequently, the upper tens' house Negroes frequently attended predominantly white churches—white Episcopal churches in particular. Many others held active memberships in predominantly white organizations. For example, a number of black Ruffins for generations patronized the arts, most notably the Boston Symphony Orchestra. What's more, they were involved in numerous civic activities that crossed racial lines with whites (Gatewood, 1990, p. 22).

Northern upper tens were usually well educated and, thus, might hold professional jobs. In addition to the various social contacts with whites, such blacks were therefore more often in contact with upper-class whites than they were with the underclass African people. Included among that number was William H. Dupree, who managed Boston's largest postal substation for many years. George L. Ruffin was a Harvard-educated lawyer who worked first as a legislator and later as a city judge. J. H. Lewis and T. A. Ridley managed large and successful clothing establishments (Gatewood, 1990). Because segregation was less of a factor, James Monroe Trotter, Dupree's brother-in-law, resided in exclusive, white-populated Hyde Park without incident. Lastly, a black Southerner named Joseph Lee from Virginia owned and operated a catering business whose clientele were the "first families of Boston." Such wealth meant that the children of the aforementioned were afforded the best educational and cultural opportunities available. Thus, Trotter's son enrolled at Harvard and one of Ruffin's sons graduated from the Massachusetts Institute of Technology, earning a degree in engineering. For their part, the wives of these upper ten men were socially active and lived quite comfortably (Gatewood, 1990).

The Boston African upper tens were more exclusive than other Northern aristocrats. Their stern disdain for the masses of dark-skinned field Negroes exceeded that of blacks in Washington, D.C., and Philadelphia. The lower classes regarded the African elite Bostonians as "cold" and "chilly" (Gatewood, 1990). In this way, Boston upper tens made sure to maintain strict boundaries between the propertied African elite and the propertyless African community. They regarded themselves by birth as superior in every way to other blacks. In particular, they saw themselves as superior to those blacks who relocated North from the South in search of work and who tended to be darker-skinned, lower-class, and uneducated. In a novel, *The Living is Easy*, Dorothy West illustrated this attitude with a complaint of one Boston upper ten: "Our fathers built a social class for us out of tailor shops and barber shops and stables and caterers' coats. We cannot afford its upkeep because they have taught us to think above their profitable oc-cupations" (quoted in Gatewood, 1990, p. 24). In the same novel, another African elite complains that "With so many of the unfortunates of our race migrating to Boston ... we find ourselves becoming crusaders for our beloved city" (quoted in Gatewood, 1990, p. 26).

Thus, as novels expressed an obvious disdain among the elite upper tens for the underclass masses, these novels also reflected a very real ten-sion that had been active within the African community since the days of the antebellum. The upper tens were so convinced of white's belief in the inferiority of African folk that they invested extra effort to differentiate themselves whenever possible. When carried to the extreme, elite blacks in Boston desired to completely deny the fact that they were African at all but rather a variation of the white population who, by wealth, education, and social poise, were no less civilized than whites.

Although the majority of upper tens were eager to separate themselves from African folk, an element of that population had sought to devote their talents and potential to uplifting the race. They were in many respects equally exclusive but recognized their responsibility to rescue the less for-tunate whose stations in life were such that no racial progress could occur. Their most noted spokesman was the first African American to earn a PhD from Harvard, William Edward Burghardt Du Bois. W. E. B. Du Bois, as he is most often known, was not from Boston but grew up in a Massachusetts city called Great Barrington. He was born of French, Indian, and African ancestry. Unlike members of the upper tens, Du Bois did not resent his Af-rican blood; his Harvard education did not motivate him to separate from the African community but, to the contrary, to uplift it.

According to Du Bois, the Negro *race* was currently a problem. The only way it might resolve its problems and improve itself would be by way of the exceptional examples of brilliant people. These people he referred to as the Talented Tenth. The Talented Tenth, according to Du Bois, represented the best within the race whose task it would be to guide the masses of poor, illiterate African members of the underclass away from the diminished elements of both the white and African races. To accomplish this monumental feat, Du Bois suggested the commitment to accomplish three necessary tasks. First, history must acknowledge that the Talented Tenth have shown themselves worthy of assuming the leadership of the African community. Secondly, blacks must acknowledge that such talented blacks must receive the best education possible. Finally, the Talented Tenth must invest their efforts to bring resolution to the so-called Negro problem. Du Bois, the greatest African intellectual in the United States, was honestly and earnestly attempting to resolve the issue of race as he saw it, which was that the problem was not the black person but instead the white racists who despised blacks, regardless from which social standing or class in society. Later, of course, Du Bois revised his notion of the Talented Tenth in an effort to secure the largest enlistment of professional blacks in the fight against illiteracy and the lack of economic development. Perhaps he recognized the elitist implications of separating from the masses would mean that the talented would not be accepted by the African community. The masses of black people resented those who saw themselves as the elite, and this could only be resolved when the professionals committed to work for the general uplift of the race.

However, there were still strong tensions between the haves and the have-nots, between the professionals who saw themselves as individuals and the blacks, whether professional, working class, or poor, who felt a need to universally transform the black community. The upper tens in the North and the aristocratic African elites in the South demonstrated even stronger allegiance to the white community, whose policies and social traditions had been responsible for their oppression. Some displayed lifestyles and traditions that reflected more of the tendencies of white folk than even those displayed by white folk. These blacks were a curious lot, whose wealth and education enabled them to fashion their lives to fit what the white community espoused should be adopted by the African community. Such Africans in every way exemplified white culture, even becoming exaggerated versions of what they perceived. Their lives were indicated by a rigid obsession with perfection that they perceived as white. Psychologist Nathan Hare (1965) referred to them as the Black Anglo-Saxons. They, more than any other, mark the political link between the antebellum house Negro African elite and the modern-day African conservative.

In his widely read *The Black Anglo-Saxons*, first published in 1965, Hare first subjected to scientific investigation the psychological dynamics of the house Negro extending to the modern-day African Conservative. He described the house Negro African aristocratic elite as "supercitizens." These blacks were reported to be even more conservative than conservative whites. However, given that African Americans in general, both then and now, were denied privileges on par with that of whites, the black elite invest all psychic energy in becoming a "super-American" in the hopes of acquiring approval and eventual acceptance by whites. By investing their psychic energy manifested in the public domain, despite having been oppressed, they display the most extreme and dramatic forms of patriotism.

Although aristocratic African elites are more often well educated, their professional status as blacks require that they be subordinate to whites who may be less skilled or formally educated. With some exceptions, house Negro elites are generally prohibited from setting up large-scale business enterprises. Thus, even those with Ivy League educations are destined to work in service fields, including being nurses, doctors, undertakers, teachers, life insurance salesmen, government clerks, social workers, and government appointees. Employed in such fields in service to the general public, whites expect them to please the white public. In response, many develop a nonchalant attitude as a defense mechanism to protect the ego from daily white insults:

I just don't let it [their status] bother me, they will declare in an effort to convince themselves as well as the listener. They affirm that you've got to be realistic, meaning that you must accept the slow pace of Negro advancement as inevitable. (Haley, 1996, p. 6)

Despite his intense efforts, the house Negro African elite can be harassed by police, ignored by taxi drivers, and discriminated against in his job. The white American public does not see him as different from the despised lowly field Negro. Because field Negroes have been known to engage in violent rebellion, the African elite, the spiritual descendant of the house Negro, is conscientious to try to prevent white folk from thinking of him as also inclined to rebel. In another attempt to buffer his ego from white public attacks, the African elite make reference to rebellious Americans of both races. In this way, he can attack his own people and rationalize African protests as the work of black "extremists," black "troublemakers," or blacks who are simply "un-American." To illustrate this, Hare references a Thanksgiving Day football game that took place in Washington, D.C. Following the game, as was frequently an occurrence, both African and white youth began rioting. Elite members of the African community took issue, criticizing the African youths and calling them "anti-American."

These black elite, through displays such as this, "[set] the race back 50 years" for those who valued catching up with the white race while never mentioning the white youth involved (Malcolm X, 1963, p. 54).

Aristocratic house Negroes abhor being labeled African or African American. They seem to prefer American Negro, Colored, or Afro American. They were never comfortable with black. In an effort to escape the denigration associated with being African, such house Negroes insist that they are American first and most importantly and then Negro second. They say, "I have left nothing in Africa." In fact, they have left their minds in Africa. They are confused, without identity that matters, and casualties of the racist propaganda wars.

At a gathering for the Association for the Study of Negro Life to raise money for the Carter G. Woodson Building program, house Negro elites purchased buttons inscribed "Proud American." Any outsiders would have thought it rather peculiar that buttons proclaiming "Proud Negro" or "Proud African" buttons were markedly absent. This pseudo-patriotism or jingoism should not be confused with authentic patriotism, in which one aims to express national loyalty by seeking the highest good for one's country. Instead, for the house Negro African elite, this is another attempt to buffer the ego from the consequences of being black in a racist society.

Black house Negro women were no less prone to the exaggerated forms of patriotism than men. Their activities also often bordered on jingoism. One such African woman, writing a column for a national Negro weekly, the *Pittsburgh Courier*, said, "We [Americans] have insulted the French nation. True, we are only being what we are—Americans" (Haley, 1996, p. 59). She then advised that we should mend our ways as the representatives of the world's leading power. At a Golden Anniversary celebration in Los Angeles, the former national president of a leading sorority of Supercitizens challenged the members to forget selfish and narrow interests and become concerned with the interests of our country and all right-thinking Americans (Haley, 1996, p. 59).

The superpatriotic African elite took every opportunity to display their identification with America and trivialize their black identity. One such black traveling in Europe complained constantly about missing the "Cokes and hot dogs" that are American staples. It is interesting that he does not miss macaroni and cheese, teacakes, sweet potato pie, or ribs, but instead he misses cokes and hot dogs. Those blacks who work for American government agencies, regardless of ranking, will often proclaim to work for some prestigious department like the Pentagon in dire hopes of making an impression, when, in fact, they may be working for some agency that services the Pentagon. Of course, today, blacks have worked for and have even run the Pentagon, but the heavy display of patriotism discussed in the 1960s by Hare is now rarely displayed. Conversely, black conservatives are among the first to wrap the flag around themselves to demonstrate that they are in sync with the white conservatives. These black conservatives are among the first to look for every instance in which Barack Obama does not wear an American flag pin. They do not weary of repeating to whomever will hear them that "I'm just an American" (Kirk, 2007), meaning that they are not a black American.

Elite house Negroes' ability to identify with America rescues them from feeling ashamed of being black or African. According to Hare, one such female confided,

> The Star Spangled Banner makes me cry. It used to make me rather uncomfortable and embarrassed. More and more, however, it chokes me up, until now it just puts knots in my stomach, clouds my eyes and sends the tears flying. (Hare, 1965, p. 67)

Aristocratic house Negroes celebrate American democracy in ways that make even disinterested onlookers curious. These black elite believe that humanity the world over is envious of American sovereignty and would immediately embrace its shores if only the opportunity would present itself. They firmly believe that in America, all men are equal and can, through hard work and discipline, realize their dreams and a better life. Accepting this mythology, some descendants of house Negroes are often heard giving thanks for slavery because they think that, through slavery, they were delivered from Africa to the American Promised Land. Thus, when media outlets report emerging democracies anywhere in Africa, the African aristocrat does not hesitate to belittle their efforts. This demonstrates not only self-hatred but also ignorance of history. Just as no Jew would ever praise God for the Shoa, there is no victory in degradation and abuse—only resilience, courage, and the willingness to defend yourself.

The house Negro African elite do not hesitate to defend the reputation of America when traveling abroad, even if it means supporting African oppression. They admonish African activists to not press too hard for civil rights at home so that they do not tarnish America in the eyes of the world regarding how America's African citizens are treated. In fact, in a message to President John F. Kennedy, African elites argued that civil rights leaders who objected to segregation were "dividing our country faster than agents of foreign powers could possibly do." Still others took issue with Kennedy for making "hasty progress" because, from their perspective, it weakened "the morale of the country." Most astonishingly, house Negro elites have mimicked the same words expressed by racist whites, who object to blacks who struggle to terminate oppression. One of the most widely spoken retorts is "Why don't you leave the country if you're so dissatisfied?"

House Negroes who are concerned about America's image abroad will not hesitate to invest personal funds to rescue it. In an effort to trivialize African discontent, they will travel solely for the purpose of alleviating the perceived urgency of combating racial discrimination so that any accusations from African Americans about their second-class citizenship will be seen as an exaggeration by those who merely seek attention or to cause trouble. On one such occasion, Hare reported a goodwill tour abroad taken by 50 members of a Negro sorority. They included African teachers, social workers, and other house Negro professionals. They stopped in eight African countries during the summer of 1962. Each traveler invested $1,798 of their personal funds for the trip—about $5,000 in today's currency. At home, other house Negro elites celebrated their trip, hailing them as ambassadors of the nation. The tour inspired the elite, who made public note of the aftermath. The *Pittsburgh Courier* reported,

> Their mere presence under these circumstances will be silent testimony to the economic and cultural status of American Negro womanhood, and will present an image which is not too often shown to African people and should be an inspiration to them. (Hare, 1965, pp. 78–79)

The house Negro elite celebrate the status of America at home as well as abroad. Local leaders complimented an elite African social club in Oklahoma City for an event they sponsored for foreign students at a nearby college. When asked to comment, the president of the organization responded that America must do more than just profess democracy to the world; instead, it must practice it, and foreign students present an opportunity for them to make the case. Thus, according to them, blacks must join whites in boasting our claims to democracy, showing that these blacks are no less American than whites. This would surely win the approval and perhaps eventual acceptance of the white community—approval that house Negro African elites so desperately crave.

Despite their attempts to solicit white approval, house Negroes' efforts have gone largely ignored. Hare reported the story of an African musician who played a benefit concert for a white university in the South. He not only ignored nearby African colleges, but he also donated $3,700 of the $5,000 fee to be paid to the white organization who invited him. However, on his way out of town, when he and his band stopped at a local restaurant to eat, they were customarily refused service. What's more, when they protested, the police were called and came prepared to make an arrest. As a result, the musician and his band were required to drive hundreds of miles before they could eat. Prior to the social revolution, it was common for blacks who protested such treatment, descendants of field Negroes, to hear that they should be careful in their dislike of injustice. Blacks who can experience such treatment and not become bitter are supposedly better adjusted than those who cannot. Conversely, psychoanalysts, including Anna Freud, contend that, in fact, it is normal to react with bitterness to a bitter situation. However, the house Negro not only suppresses his bitterness but is more likely to take pride in the fact that, by this act, they are not prejudiced, as if this somehow elevates them to or above the status of whites. They deceive themselves and, thus, psychologically deny objective reality. They are motivated by the desire to acquire white approval, no matter the cost to themselves or African people in general.

Occasional gestures of integration deceive the contemporary descendant of the elite house Negro, thereby further motivating his tendency to conform and exaggerate patriotism. He is content to accept that he is well adjusted and esteemed to the extent he can escape his blackness, and this drives him further away from himself. The white community compliments and praises politically the house Negro for his disorientation. Such Africans have succeeded in denouncing their blackness, which otherwise they believe would compromise their material success. They can, therefore, be of no use to their own communities because they are frightened about the possibility of losing the little space they have gained in the corporation, university, and political or business circles. They are victims, pinned against the walls of their own ignorance and the arrogance of white racial symbolic domination. The irony is that these house Negroes then consider themselves more capable of seeing both sides of whatever issue when, in fact, they merely look at all facets of an issue to discover how they might become less African and more white, which, in American politics, is conservative!

## Psychological Domination

The enduring characteristic of any enslavement is domination, and the most salient part of domination warping the mental territory of the dominated. The making of the house Negro was as much an action of the white power elite as it was the submission of the African. Of course, the one element that bound the white slave master and the African was violence. In every aspect of his or her life, the African was violated physically and psychologically. Violence orchestrated against African women and men was at the center of the enslavement. In its rawest form, the abuse of the workers, the mutilation of the insolent, the crippling of the strong, the rape of black women—all of whom were considered chattel—were the principal means by which the slave master ensured that blacks who worked in the house would be psychologically dominated. Thus, the severity of the physical domination of enslaved Africans was equaled only by the psychological domination. One type of oppression impacted the physical quality of life among the enslaved, and the other form of oppression influenced the psychological quality of life. Both forms devastated the African and created enormous crises in action and thinking. Contemporary writers rarely consider the implications of 246 years of racial brutality.

The vast majority of Africans who worked in the fields, often apart from whites except the overseers, came to view the condition of enslavement as the worst form of hell. They had no individual liberty and no collective sense of freedom for a people whose long history had always been one of complete openness to the universe, the environment, and the family. When such individual and collective control over one's own life and family was terminated, liberty was killed and the African personality became mangled. Field Negroes, therefore, were forced into a political and social unity, regardless of ethnic group or previous social class, to become a resistance phalanx against all physical and mental assaults against the masses. This was the beginning of a common front, often impenetrable for the house Negro, to combat undifferentiated abuse and death. Here was born the group, the idea that individuals could not save the group but rather only the group could save the group. Here also was the birth of organization in the interest of common advancement. If a person needed spiritual, psychological, or physical healing, the field Negroes developed among themselves specialized talents to aid one another apart from the white world. Secret knowledge and concealed assistance were often at the base of the trust that was necessary to create organization.

Quite exceptionally, the field Negroes recognized individual gifts and geniuses of spirit and courage but also understood that such gifts had to be used for group survival because no African could survive solely as an individual. All were oppressed by the same system and all were considered inferior beings designed to carry out the duties forced on them by whites. There was no individuality or personhood respected by whites. Thus, freedom as a concept was nourished in America by Africans who, experiencing collective bondage, forged the fight for freedom and claimed it as a greater good than individual liberty because it was a quest for everyone to reach a collective goal of complete liberation. It became the standard by which all African Americans' organizations were judged, even after the end of the enslavement.

African Americans were enslaved much longer than we have been free. In the following discussion, we turn our attention to examine the nature of the psychological brutality that jeopardized identity and self-worth. We shall do this by discussing erasing memory, scarring the African psyche, and separating enslaved Africans from their own essential cultural mythologies. Indeed, because stability and consistency in the Africans' world was destroyed, they suffered mental chaos, which then led to further erosion of a sense of belonging.

### Loss of Memory

Because it is commonplace that the loss of memory is one of the elements in making a person a slave, we must examine how that condition occurred among Africans. Wiping one's memory during the inception of perpetual slavery of Africans in the Americas was not a subtle process; instead; it was quite severe. You had to lose your name. You could no longer be known by the name of your clan, ethnic group, or family, but were *made* to become something entirely different in name. Thus, slaves were made, not born; even though one might be born into the system of enslavement, even here we would have to speak about the nature of the making of a slave as something that was deliberate and violent. Robbing a person of his name is no simple act; it is something that reaches to the depth of a person's humanity. When you have lost your name, you are a victim of the worst possible loss of memory. It is bad enough that your name is stolen, but along with your family's name, your mother's name and your father's name have also been robbed from you. Indeed, all of the achievements of a hundred generations are wiped out in the cruel process of taking your original name and giving you a name worthy of an enslaved person, a name that has no more significance in the arena of your past history. You are like a "motherless child." Hassimi Maiga wrote of this in his major work on Songhay culture (Maiga, 2008, pp. 3–25). The person who was captured in warfare or was orphaned became integrated into the conquering group but referred to as "the one without a mother."

The plantation was where the most insidious types of control and manipulation occurred. Because the house Negroes were not as numerous on plantations as the field Negroes, whites often manipulated and propagandized them more severely. The plantation owners used pet names for their house Negroes, similar to those they would give to their favorite dogs and cats, and this made the house Negroes feel close to the master. Terms of endearment like Penny, Pee Wee, Le Roi, and Plenty were often used to refer to the whites' favorite enslaved Africans. Whites taught the house Negroes that they were different from the masses of Negroes, so they often felt much closer to whites than to other blacks. They would probably tell the slave owner that they couldn't stand such-and-such black person, confirming for the slave owner his own opinion about that black person. The reality was, however, that they were enslaved whereas whites were not; regardless, the conditioning for the plantation oppression created a separation between the house Negroes and the field Negroes that was to last through the end of the enslavement.

Imagine a child who is born into a family with well-understood and long-lasting traditions and values who then forgets his traditions when he is confronted by new circumstances. He forgets his mother and father and cannot remember the names of his aunts and uncles. He even forgets the name of his place of birth. He becomes lost in the midst of other people, perhaps even envying the memory of others because he cannot remember his own sense of place.

## *Mental Impact on Africans*

Living in the master's house did not come without a price for house Negroes. The better clothes they wore and finer foods they ate created a distorted sense of reality. Having been separated from the masses and made to feel valuable because of the master's favor, the house Negroes convinced themselves that they were somehow better than their counterparts in the fields. Many of them, having white physical features, could successfully escape and start a new life as poor whites, perhaps claiming to be Portuguese or Spanish. Male house Negroes in particular were given to such escapes from slavery because, having white facial features, they could pass for white with relative ease and enter the mainstream of white society. They could relocate to another town or leave the South altogether. Once safely settled, they might find a job, take a white bride, and start a family without ever revealing the details of their racial heritage. In fact, there are no pure races on the earth; indeed, African blood entered the white family tree in America about as early as European blood entered the African family in America. We are essentially an interracial nation. The problem, of course, with the house Negro is that he saw "white blood" as being superior to African blood, following the same inane line of thinking that the slave owners transmitted to him.

Passing for white was less of an option for house Negro women who lived under the master's roof because white women were often required to establish the biological details of their background as a measure to keep the white race pure. "Lily white" was not just a metaphor for skin color but for blood as well. Whites assumed that those who could not prove their total whiteness were morally tainted and, therefore, ineligible for a decent marriage. In fact, the white-looking black women, by remaining among the African population, frequently gained higher status in the class hierarchy. However, both male and female house Negroes were more intimately associated with the master's forms of domination than the field Negroes. The house Negroes had come to believe that to gain the respect and dignity they so deeply desired, they had to appeal to the master's good nature politically. After the end of the enslavement, no one African American did more to make this point than Booker T. Washington. In a heroic attempt to lift the status of blacks in the South, Washington displayed an unyielding desire to embrace the politics of his master's domination. He would become what the white man desired: a subservient person seeking to please white people rather than fight for political and education equality.

## The Washington Example

Booker T. Washington was one of the most complex of the African American leaders. He was born in 1856 on a tobacco plantation in Virginia. His mother was a house Negro—a cook—and his father was said to be a white man from a neighboring farm. In his famous autobiography, *Up from Slavery*, Washington revealed the complications of his status as the child of a house Negro. Although his mother may have been favored by the slave master, James Burroughs, she still suffered at the hands of the slave owner. Washington never forgot the pain he saw in his mother's eyes nor the attitude that field Negroes had toward his mother because they believed that she was in a higher or better position because she was in the white man's house.

Education was never an option for black children. However, Washington got a chance to go to school when he was ordered to carry the books of one of the slave owner's daughters. School made a significant impression on him, and he felt that he needed to go to school for himself one day. When he recalled this experience in his book, he felt it was like thinking about going to paradise.

After the Confederacy was defeated, all the enslaved Africans on the Burroughs' plantation were assembled and told they were free. Some chose to remain on the property, but others left. Booker's mother left the plantation and took her family to Malden, West Virginia, in search of her black husband, Booker's stepfather. Numerous black men raised as their own children the offspring of white men who had raped black women.

Washington wanted to prove to his stepfather and mother that he was grateful for having a family who loved him. When he was 10, he took a job in the salt mine, going to work at 4 a.m. so that he could then go to the black school later in the day. A wealthy white woman took him in as a houseboy after he had worked and studied diligently, and she made him responsible for keeping her house. Thus, after slavery was over, there were still Africans who were considered house Negroes. Washington's time as a houseboy may have laid the foundation for his analysis of the white idea about domination. He learned what to say and what not to say if he wanted to maintain his position in the house. He mastered the technique of managing other Africans in the interest of whites. As his mother had been a cook and his biological father a white man, Washington seemed to have mastered the necessary behavior to be a useful houseboy. But he was not satisfied. He could not see himself carrying out the will of the whites forever without seeking to raise the living conditions of his own people. One might say that Booker T. Washington had a conscience and could not or would not allow his own situation to make him acquiesce to the oppression of blacks. But his most daunting challenge was determining how to save Africans from the vilest and most obscene forms of white aggression while at the same time making economic progress.

By the age of 16, Washington had decided to walk nearly 500 miles to Hampton Institute, a school that had been founded for Africans and Indians. When the 16-year-old boy entered the campus with his ragged clothes, looking like a tramp, the head mistress of the school was shocked. He pleaded with her to grant him admission to the school. Once she had tested his ability to sweep a room clean and to be disciplined, she accepted him as a student.

Washington excelled at Hampton, adding as much value to the school as he received from it. He even became one of the star instructors at the Institute. Later, when a group of blacks wanted a school in Tuskegee, they contacted the administrators at Hampton, who agreed that Washington was the man for the job. He went to Alabama and founded Tuskegee Institute as a young educator of 25 years of age. In just a few years, he would be considered the most well-known black educator in the United States.

Washington believed that every day should be filled with some work. He once remarked that there was never a time of his life that was devoted to play. Furthermore, he would remind his audiences and readers that for almost every day of his life, he was engaged in some form of labor. Self-reliance was the foundation for his social philosophy.

To speak of Booker T. Washington as a descendant of the house Negro syndrome suggests that he was not ready to confront racism and white racial domination head-on. He wanted peace, believing that peace would allow the black race to prepare for assuming fuller, more powerful positions in the future. Thus, he cautioned against voting rights protests and demands, campaigns for equality, and interracial education. According to Washington, the white man was hopelessly a bigot who would never relinquish the idea that he was superior to the black man, and therefore, the numerically smaller population of blacks could not possibly secure equal rights. What he wanted for the blacks in the South and, perhaps, in the nation was domestic indispensability.

Washington's philosophy was sealed in his Atlanta Compromise Speech in 1895, when he spoke to the largely white audience at the Atlanta Exposition. In the address, he said that whites and blacks could be as one as the hand in all things essential to mutual progress, but in all things purely social they would be as separate as the fingers. Indeed, Washington placed the idea of the separation prior to his statement about "one as the hand." Those who attacked his philosophy called it accommodationist. Some of the major African American thinkers and philosophers challenged his view of the American nation, but, nevertheless, Washington remained a paramount black leader in the eyes of the whites of his day. He died in 1915, but prior to his death at 59, he had condemned the movie *Birth of a Nation*, contributed to a nationalistic black movement, organized black industrial groups, and worked for the liberation of the Congo Free State.

# CHAPTER FOUR

# The Conservative Political Agenda

The agenda of the black conservatives mirrors that of the white conservatives in many respects. However, at the base of the black conservative political agenda is a self-hating turnkey. They are effectively against anything that the Civil Rights Movement accomplished—a movement that made it possible for them to be, in many cases, professional conservative pundits. Prior to this movement so identified with the descendants of the field Negroes, there were no black conservative pundits on the political platforms supported by whites. The black conservatives' agenda appears to equate essentially to oppressing African Americans. In the history of black conservatism, they have neither fought for collective liberation nor asserted constructive arguments against the white domination of the black population. Instead, the agenda is composed of only self-interest, personal ambition without regard to the masses, and shame. The problem is that black conservatives have rarely been good historians and have seldom explored the ramifications of domination on the psychological views of blacks or whites.

America has never been a homogeneous nation; it has always had population diversity despite the early whites' intent to make it a white nation. However, America is less homogeneous now than at any other time in its history. When Barack Obama was elected president of the United States in 2008, he had risen to the top of a nation that, just a few years earlier, would have condemned him as a tragic mulatto. Nevertheless, preserving the fundamental white conservative agenda continued after Obama was elected. Of course, for the most part, Europeans who first arrived in the New World took full advantage of creating an environment where the mere fact of Caucasian race ancestry was seen as a birthright to a host of opportunities necessarily denied to others. Enslaved Africans in particular, even after the Civil War, were denied the most basic rights and opportunities associated with their newfound citizenship because of the contrast in their skin color compared to members of the mainstream white population. Thus, the Irish and Italians also experienced various forms of prejudice and discrimination when they arrived as immigrants. Once they became citizens, however, by the second or third generation, these European immigrants secured permanently their status as first-class, mainstream Americans. They could now enjoy the privileges of the status quo, having overcome their immigrant category to become truly white.

Even if the desire to become white had appeared in some psychologically aberrant way among African people who were readily identifiable by skin color as black, it still would have demonstrated the insidious nature of racism. During the antebellum period, blacks who sought to become whites sacrificed any lifestyle advantages on the altar of white violence against all blacks—light complexioned or not. This was brought to the public and legal eye when, around the end of the 19th century, Homer Plessy, a fair-skinned black man, would be forced off of a public train in Louisiana when he was testing the idea of color discrimination.

Plessy was a 30-year-old shoemaker who lived in New Orleans in 1892 when the city and the state were still smarting from Louisiana blacks' activism. On June 7, Plessy was put in jail for sitting in the "whites only" car on the East Louisiana Railroad Line. Because Plessy was only one-eighth black and, thus, seven-eighths white, he went to court to argue that the Louisiana law titled the Separate Car Act was in violation of the U.S. Constitution's 13th and 14th Amendments. However, according to the state, Plessy was legally black, regardless of the number of white ancestors he had, and, therefore, had to sit in the "colored" section of the train. The case was heard by Judge John Howard Ferguson, who had been a lawyer in Massachusetts and who had once declared the Separate Car Act unconstitutional on the grounds that any train that ran through several states was no longer under the jurisdiction of a single state. However, in Plessy's case, the judge agreed that the state could regulate railroad companies that operated only within Louisiana. Plessy was found guilty of refusing to leave the whites-only area of the train. In 1896 the defendant appealed to the U.S. Supreme Court, which also found Plessy guilty. Justice Henry Brown wrote for the seven-person majority:

> A statute which implies merely a legal distinction between the white and colored races—a distinction which is founded in the color of the two races, and which must also exist so long as white men are distinguished from the other race by color—has a tendency to destroy the legal equality of the two races ... the object of the 14th Amendment was undoubtedly to enforce the absolute equality of the two races before the law, but in the nature of things it could not have been intended to abolish distinctions based upon color or to enforce social, as distinguished from political equality, or a commingling of the two races upon terms unsatisfactory to either. (Brown 1958, pp. 50–51)

One member of the Supreme Court, Justice John Harlan, dissented, writing,

> Our Constitution is color-blind, and neither knows nor tolerates classes among citizens. In respect of civil rights, all citizens are equal before the law.... In my opinion, the judgment this day rendered will, in time, prove to be quite as pernicious as the decision made by this tribunal in the Dred Scott Case.... The present decision, it may well be apprehended, will not only stimulate aggressions, more or less brutal and irritating, upon the admitted rights of colored citizens, but will encourage the belief that it is possible, by means of state enactments, to defeat the beneficent purposes which the people of the United States had in view when they adopted the recent amendments of the Constitution. (Brown, 1958, 50–51)

Justice Harlan's dissent was prophetic, as whites created separate facilities all over the nation as "separate but equal" schools, shops, railroad cars, theaters, restrooms, and restaurants. Of course, almost none of these facilities were equal. Whites always received the best facilities, the best schools, and the best public parks. The Plessy decision had set a precedent that would not be overturned until the Supreme Court's *Brown v. Topeka Board of Education* decision in 1954, which struck down the separate but equal doctrine.

The *Brown v. Topeka Board of Education* case turned on a young third grader named Linda Brown who had to walk a mile across several railroad tracks to a black school even though a white school was only seven blocks away. When her father, Oliver Brown, tried to enroll her at the white school, the principal refused. At that point, Oliver Brown asked the head of the Topeka branch of the National Association for the Advancement of Colored People (NAACP) to assist the family in challenging the segregation of public schools. In 1951 the NAACP requested an injunction that would prevent the segregation of the public schools. The U.S. District Court for Kansas heard the case. The NAACP argued that the segregated schools sent the message that white students were superior to black students and that, therefore, black students were inferior to white students. However, the court ruled in favor of the Board of Education, contending that the *Plessy v. Ferguson* ruling had decided that schools could be separate but equal. The NAACP then took the case to the U.S. Supreme Court. The Supreme Court heard the case in 1952 but did not come to a final decision until May 17, 1954, after re-argumentation that segregation deprived black children of equal protection of the law. Chief Justice Earl Warren read the unanimous decision:

> We come then to the question presented: Does segregation of children in public schools solely on the basis of race, even though the physical facilities and other "tangible" factors may be equal, deprive the children of the minority group of equal educational opportunities? We believe that it does.... We conclude that in the field of public education the doctrine of "separate but equal" has no place. Separate educational facilities are inherently unequal. Therefore, we hold that the plaintiffs and others similarly situated for whom the actions have been brought are, by reason of the segregation complained of, deprived of the equal protection of the laws guaranteed by the Fourteenth Amendment. (Ziegler, 1958, pp. 78–79)

Thus, the Supreme Court set aside the doctrine of "separate but equal" of the *Plessy v. Ferguson* case. This meant that schools across the country would have to desegregate. This ruling also declared the mandatory segregation that existed in 21 states unconstitutional.

Of course, although *Plessy v. Ferguson* was struck down by the U.S. Supreme Court, the underlying idea giving rise to the earlier doctrine of separate but equal and also the original framing of the debate around two races, in which "one drop of African blood makes you black," remained a part of American popular culture. Therefore, racism had not been obliterated.

Thus, whiteness remained the standard color of the law. Initially, the Constitution allowed only propertied white males to vote. By denying the right to vote to all but propertied white males, white males maintained exclusively the power and, thus, the authority to determine quality of life. Americans who did not belong to this demographic group were forced to negotiate with them for *some* of their privilege. Propertied white males' ability to exercise power and influence in the affairs of the nation is the practical genesis of conservative politics in modern-day America (McIntosh, 1990).

The political conservative agenda seeks to maintain white privilege in all dimensions of American society because the conservative sees the United States as a white nation with white values. There is even now no leading American conservative voice that champions the rights of African Americans, Latinos, or Native Americans. Indeed, they have rarely assumed leadership on issues of women's rights, gay rights, or rights of the physically challenged. Those who accept such a view of American society often express fear that multiculturalism, immigration, and the doctrine of openness to others will dilute America. They worry that English will no longer be the dominant language in the United States or about the rising tide of Mexican and Latinos immigrants from other places in the Americas. Race often appears to be an unspoken factor in conservative political discourse, regardless of whether they are white or black. Thus, the legacy of the house Negro, whose identification with the slave master is complete, unbreakable, solid, might be seen in contemporary politics as well ("Colin Powell: Bush's all-American house Negro," 2002, October 16).

The election of President Barack Obama further worried many conservatives, especially the so-called media gangsters who use the airwaves to spout many inane and inflammatory comments about blacks, Latinos, gay and lesbian people, and immigrants. They saw Obama's election as an attempt on the part of the liberal Left to steal the center from the Right. Indeed, many conservative pundits declared that because Obama had been elected president, the country had transcended race, so now it no longer needed to be discussed in America. Of course, this was not so, and of all Americans, they knew the lie they were espousing best of all. Obama's election to the presidency depended greatly on the black vote: more than

97 percent of blacks voted for Obama. Meanwhile, less than 50 percent of the white voters chose Obama. Clearly he was the choice of the African American population. Fortunately for Obama, although he received fewer white votes than Senator John McCain, he did receive enough white votes combined with his numbers from African, Asian, and Latino Americans to win the election.

The black community generally accepts that African conservatives may succeed with whites after these black conservatives have demonstrated their willingness to put forth an extra effort to secure white privilege. Despite racial disadvantages they themselves have experienced, many African conservatives believe that the best road for African Americans is to follow the path of white conservatism. They assume that the values espoused by white conservatives would eradicate all disadvantages blacks suffer. Not only have black conservatives been wrong in such a naïve analysis, but they have also demonstrated a severe misreading of American history, which, had they looked more closely, would have shown them that race was a much more defining factor in determining advantage than they cared to discuss.

The values articulated by black conservatives include:

> Supporting the right to own guns
> Supporting competition in work
> Supporting self-defense
> Rejecting the deification of government
> Downplaying disparities in wealth
> Refusing to complain but instead taking personal action to help situations
> Refusing to insist on "mindless" equality

In effect, the black conservatives believe that combating *lust, laziness, jealousy, gluttony, pride, corruption,* and *credulity* can be achieved by these values. Obviously, the African conservatives have bought into the idea that human beings are responsible for their conditions. They cannot see the impact of superstructure, ideology, environment, and laws on blacks, women, or the poor. In fact, they would rather blame the victims than suggest that ideologies like patriarchy, racism, homophobia, anti-immigrationism, inequality in education, and hegemony have anything to do with the present human condition.

The problem for the conservatives is that they had hoped that Obama would express their brand of exceptionalism once he became president. In fact, they wanted him to be held up as proof that there was no longer racism in America. He was Harvard educated and a family man—the precise symbol of progress that they could use to try to prove that blacks could make it in America if only they work hard. This is always the intent of those who want to undermine the disadvantaged and those who have suffered discrimination: Blame the victim. But as Brent Staples (2009, pp. 2–15) stated in an article about Obama and race, "He has made it clear that the election of the first African American president, while noteworthy in a nation built on the backs of slaves, did not signal a sudden, magical end to discrimination." For example, S. Allen Counter is a Harvard Medical School professor who was arrested at his house and hauled off to the Cambridge Police Headquarters nearly three years prior to the high-profile arrest of Henry Louis Gates, Jr. Counter believes even now that his arrest was racial harassment (Jan 2009, August 6). When journalists asked President Obama about the arrest of his friend Henry Louis Gates, Jr., in his own house, by the Cambridge police, the president commented on the tendency of some police to use racial profiling. In the case of the Cambridge policeman who arrested Professor Gates, President Obama said that the officer "acted stupidly." Staples summed up his comments about the president aptly: "People who have heretofore viewed Mr. Obama as a post-racial abstraction were no doubt surprised by these remarks. This could be because they were hearing him fully for the first time" (Graham, 2009, July 22). As much as some whites and blacks wanted to make Obama's election a statement for black exceptionalism, the newly elected president rejected the role, believing firmly, as black conservatives seem not to at times, that racism is still a problem in American society.

The venerable Harry Belafonte sparked a controversy during an interview in October 2002 on California radio station KFMB when he was asked about the then–Secretary of State, Colin Powell. Belafonte said,

There's an old saying in the days of slavery, there are those enslaved Africans who lived on the plantation, and there were those enslaved Africans who lived in the house. You got the privilege of living in the house if you served the master to exactly the way the master intended to have you serve him. That gave you privilege. Colin Powell is permitted to come into the house of the master, as long as he will serve the master according to the master's dictates. Now, when Colin Powell dares to suggest something other than what the master wants to hear, he will be turned back out to pasture. ("Colin Powell: Bush's all-American house Negro," 2002, October 16)

Beyond the volatile nature of Belafonte's comments is a kernel of truth in the political parallels between historical and contemporary times. The house Negro was essentially powerless, although powerful whites protected him. In contemporary times, whites look at the African person who is charged with running an aspect of the empire with suspicion unless he can interpret his actions through the prism of the master's vision. To have one's own vision, especially if this vision is a critique of the white vision, is to risk danger.

This willingness to have one's own vision is complicated by the modern-day conservative obsession with a moral code based entirely on a white Christian Anglo-Saxon ideology. Blaming the victim for their oppressive circumstances is the most convenient way that this white, church-going community can rescue its conscience from the consequences of oppressive actions. As a result, when the conservative views African people as power-less, lazy, or corrupt, this is usually a sign that the viewer sees Africans as inferior, and therefore, the opinion is a rationalization for the victimization of the African. Under the circumstances, this creates a cycle of political turmoil, which means that racial conflict in America is bound for a long life if not, as Derrick Bell predicted, permanence. That is because the African people and human beings in general do not want to be dominated in any fashion. Freedom is an essential human quest, regardless of race. Politi-cally, the resulting conflict encourages opposition and suspicion of others' intentions, particularly if they are members of another racial group. When repeated, without any historical break, the political boundaries between right and wrong begin to blur. Enabled by religion, white conservatives in particular are seduced by moral justification and see no need for objective investigation of conservative policies. Thus, victims themselves are often among the advocates of this philosophy.

African conservatives have assumed a vital role in maintaining white hegemonic politics as they take up the mantle of explaining the ideologies of individualism and free-wheeling capitalism. These blacks are creations of the social and political backlashes to the advances African Americans made during the 1960s Civil Rights Movement. Whites felt besieged and surrounded by blacks, who had risen with indignation to challenge the segregation, discrimination, and prejudice found in society. The white backlash found expression through white political organizations that pushed for a conservative agenda as they sought to shore up what they thought was a losing side against the integration and progressive movements of liberal whites and blacks. The success of these white conservatives shocked both the emerging liberal elements as well as the black Civil Rights Movement. In many respects, the black progressives had attacked the liberals, thus weakening their stand against the white conservatives. Disavowing many of the actions and statements of liberal whites who, according to blacks, did not want to relinquish their roles as paternalists and maternalists to the black movement, the black leadership did not anticipate the quick rise of the white reactionaries. What's more, the black Civil Rights leaders could not have predicted that black conservatives would appear to stand side by side with the white conservatives.

Discrimination continues to be one of the most potent political factors of life for African Americans despite all of the political and social changes achieved over the past thirty years (Kitano, 1985). Furthermore, any discussion of the impact of discrimination in the lives of blacks and whites reveals that whites benefit from discrimination against blacks on every level, including education, occupation, income, and, more importantly, power and status. Even when power at the highest level of government has changed, the overall status of blacks still tends to be affected by racism. That is significant because a lack of general power may have severe consequences for quality of life, as stated by Pinkney (1975):

> Chief among the characteristics of the urban African community are its powerlessness and its dependence on the frequently hostile white community which surrounds it. These enclaves are kept powerless by powerful individuals and institutions in the white community. The dwellings of the urban African community are usually owned by absentee white landlords and institutions, and no attempt is made to maintain the buildings or to provide the customary services to their inhabitants. Residential buildings, for which the occupants are charged high rents, frequently do not provide safe and adequate shelter. Often they are owned by wealthy and politically prominent suburban residents.

Therefore, discrimination is well established in America, especially given that the initial role of African Americans as enslaved workers was merely to serve the larger white community for whatever reasons and by any means necessary. For this to be sustained in the modern era requires white Americans to maintain discriminatory practices so that blacks accept the decisions made for them from authorities outside the African community. During the antebellum era, blacks who objected to such oppression could be easily brought back in line because, aside from violence, they were segregated on the plantation and elsewhere in society.

History has taught us that discrimination against one group by another does not occur without costs to human interaction. The most obvious of these is the destructive roles played by prejudice and discrimination in the conservative political agenda. Prejudice and discrimination are necessary to assure inequality in order to maintain control of the masses. Both African and white conservatives insist that prejudice is a matter of history and is no longer relevant in the lives of American citizens. However, research from public opinion polls, such as that conducted by Thomas Pavlak, indicates this is not the case (1976). Pavlak's poll suggests that the most accurate measure of inequality is intermarriage, which the majority of whites continue to oppose when the potential spouse is black rather than, say, Asian or Native American.

To maintain the façade of political and social equality, white racism requires the use of code words and code behaviors that are used to mask obvious racial inequality that is no longer fashionable. Thus, without commenting directly, the conservative rhetoric can carry hidden messages that are couched in terms understood by the conservative faithful. Conservatives oppose issues such as affirmative action and busing, for example, and the reasons stated for this opposition have nothing whatsoever to do with race or discrimination. In fact, the basis of conservative political activity, which insists on the most fundamental conservative values, seems to be the desire to exploit others. The ability to exploit assumes that if a person could prevail against others, then his or her problems, wants, needs, and desires would be solved and satisfied. Part of this assumption is related to the fact that one needs power to prevail against those who are not members of one's own group. Thus, in order to exploit and discriminate against others in any sense, power must be obtained, and once acquired, it becomes the positive reinforcement for continued exploitation. Under these circumstances, we can see that the conservative mindset views liberal politics not as a struggle of blacks for equality but simply as a loss of power for whites.

The modern-day conservative political agenda represents a potent means of discrimination by which the African community remains under plantation-like control. Although the legalized slavery of Africans ended in 1865, the impact of the experience continues to affect the political dynamics between whites and blacks to this day. Although it is a less examined issue, the modern-day political implications of slavery have become an increasingly relevant dynamic in recent years. Unfortunately, if the African community considers the multitude of books and magazines devoted to the study of civic affairs, there remain both African and white scholars of the social sciences who have not the slightest inclinations to study African political participation as it pertains to strengthening the American nation.

The modern conservative era, actually initiated under President Ronald Reagan, trivialized the significance of the African presence in society (Reeves, 2005). Antagonism against Black Studies reached a fever pitch during the Reagan years, and since that time, conservative pundits have used code terms such as *special interests* and *group rights* to characterize their position regarding African Americans who seek changes in our social and political conditions. Whether the topic is education, health care, or police interactions, the conservatives argue that the discourse should be about patriotism and not about the interests of one group or another. Mass media, dominated by the post-Reagan political machine, failed for a long time to adequately assess the nature of the discourse.

Increasingly, however, society has understood the political distractions utilized by black and white conservative radio hosts—the leading "intellectuals" of the politics of exclusion. They do not want any more immigrants and they do not want to open or extend the freedoms of the land to other people. Black conservatives have also fought against affirmative action as well as the increase of opportunity for women and Mexican immigrants. They have often become the subterranean forces for the political Right.

We see these black conservatives as contemporary representatives of the antebellum house Negroes (Felix, 2005). Even with all the attention given to them by the conservative establishment, black conservatives have become irrelevant to the struggle to eliminate discrimination, and they are more isolated than ever from the mainstream of African American political thought. Furthermore, they have not been able to effect any real changes in society because of their positions in the master's house.

For many reasons, the political role of African conservatives in exploiting the larger African community has remained an embarrassing blot on the conservative movement. African conservatives have gained no traction among the descendants of the field Negroes. They are marginalized because most blacks see them as oppressing African people and, as with antebellum "house Negroes," they see themselves as being apart from or above the masses. They would never refer to themselves as Africans, preferring to call themselves colored or Negro to reflect the historical usages of their masters.

Most house Negroes experienced psychological disorientation. They knew neither their names nor their ethnic identities. They resented their mothers and fathers who were often field Negroes except when they were the offspring of the white master. In a contemporary sense, most house Negroes understood nothing of their own history and had a limited relationship with their cultural history. They are, therefore, victims who either have never had any thoughts about Africans as human beings or have had that information erased. Consequently, they are disoriented. They may even claim to dislike being identified as black or African. They would much rather identify with the attitudes and orientations of the white world. This attitude explains how they are able to manufacture information and arguments to continue to exploit Africans.

\* \* \*

Political conservatism carries with it the idea of preserving the status quo. A special characteristic of it, however, according to Philip Agre, is that it is undemocratic (2004, p. 2). Agre stated that "Conservatism is the domination of society by an aristocracy." For this reason, conservatism is incompatible with democracy because it is "a destructive system of inequality and prejudice that is founded on deception and has no place in the modern world" (2004, p. 2). Agre contended that disdain for the democratic system from an objective perspective is, therefore, the essence of the conservative political agenda because democracy is coincident with change. Subsequently, an objective perspective of conservatism should require that society be structured in the form of an aristocratic hierarchy, wherein domination is the forte of the most powerful, that is, white race aristocracy (Agre, 2004, p. 3).

The modern-day African conservative represents a corrupted version of the "American Dream." Although no less talented than their plantation forebears, their criticism of the African people has placed the modern-day African conservative at the forefront of media and academic prestige (Toppo, 2005). The Bush presidential administration paid one such African conservative a substantial sum to sway African Americans' reactions to the failed education program "No Child Left Behind" (Toppo, 2005). In an attempt to recruit support, conservatives awarded more than a quarter million dollars to this African political pundit to promote their policies on his nationally syndicated television show. After depositing monies into his personal accounts, this African conservative was urged by white conservatives to recruit other blacks who would similarly appreciate receiving such compensation. Fortunately, the culprit was exposed, and he then immediately went "underground" to escape public scrutiny.

"No Child Left Behind" was an education program established under the administration of George W. Bush that emphasized testing teachers and students without providing enough funds to the schools, and it was part of a conservative political agenda. Among the most polarizing of policies not associated with the conservative political agenda is Affirmative Action.

The idea of Affirmative Action has irritated the conservative movement for decades and divided the population in many cases along racial lines. Nowhere was that division more evident than at the University of Michigan a few years ago, when students erupted into heated protest ignited by the anticipated visit of the African conservative Ward Connerly to their Ann Arbor campus. This African conservative from California was scheduled to deliver his anti–Affirmative Action message to a largely African audience in hopes of getting the policy eliminated as an admissions tool. Of course, to the dismay of many white Americans and most black conservatives, the majority of respected political scientists agree that African Americans are more likely to be politically liberal when it comes to Affirmative Action and other racial issues. Spurred on by conservative support, black conservatives have not hesitated to publicly criticize not only liberal policies such as Affirmative Action but also African icons of the Civil Rights Movement, including Jesse Jackson, Al Sharpton, Martin Luther King, Jr., and others. Many such critics are funded by white conservative think tanks similar to those who funded the "No Child Left Behind" policy, which attempted to mislead the African people.

The legislation enacted by Congress to ensure equality for women and African people/of color did not originate with Affirmative Action (Hamilton, 1989). In fact, according to Congress (1935), the original concept of Affirmative Action was meant to benefit nonunionized, white males who sought redress for discrimination by employers. One of its primary sponsors was a New York Senator named Robert F. Wagner (U.S. Congress, July 5, 1935). During a session of the 74th Congress, it was declared that discrimination against an employee by an employer shall require "such person to cease and desist from such unfair labor practice, and to take such affirmative action, including reinstatement of employees with or without back pay, as will effectuate the policies of this act" (U.S. Congress, July 5, 1935). Formally known as the National Labor Relations Act—public law 198, and commonly referred to as the Wagner Act, Congress approved it on July 5, 1935. The original language ignored discrimination against women and African people/of color; the blatant sexism and overt racism that was characteristic of the time made those concerns a moot point. "Employee" was understood by all to refer to white males, preferably of non-Jewish stock. This legislation marked the beginning of Affirmative Action in America. Its central tenet was that it is not enough to cease and desist discriminatory acts; the consequences of historical injustices require deliberate action to be corrected. The Wagner Act of 1935 intended to correct past injustices by posting notices of a new policy and reinstating workers to good standing who were fired for union activity (Gorin, 1983). Had this law not corrected injustices, the future influence of employers' past physical and financial intimidation would have distorted any democratic processes in support of the workers. It benefited white males who had been discriminated against, eventually eliminating the problem completely. Critics of the day did not attack it as "preferential treatment" or "reverse discrimination" against employers but instead recognized its value to society.

Affirmative Action remained law, but was largely ignored after union successes, particularly among industrial workers (U.S. Congress, July 5, 1935). Employment discrimination continued, but in a different context several decades later. Civil Rights activists demanded that employers be held accountable for discriminatory practices such as hiring workers, particularly white males, by word-of-mouth referrals, which meant that a racist employer with an all-white, all-male work force would probably continue to have an all-white, all-male work force, even after ceasing discrimination against new applicants (Hamilton, 1989). Under such circumstances, new applicants would likely be the relatives and friends of existing employees. The effects of the past would theoretically perpetuate, even following legislation making discrimination illegal. At the insistence of political activists, during the 92nd Congress, Affirmative Action passed as the Equal Employment Opportunity Act on March 24, 1972 (U.S. Senate 97th Congress, First Session, 1981, May 4, June 11, 18 & July 16). The Act stated, "affirmative action as may be appropriate, may include, but is not limited to, reinstatement or hiring of employees, with or without back pay, or any other equitable relief as the court deems appropriate." The gender and racial context of this most recent interpretation intended the policy to benefit women and people of color primarily, that is, the African population. Its impact extended far beyond industrial employers into universities and various governmental agencies (U.S. Congress, March 24, 1972). It sustained the spirit of the Wagner Act, which had contended that to eliminate discrimination only at the decision-making point would not eliminate it in the future because of past practices. Therefore, the 92nd Congress determined that affirmative action of some kind was indeed necessary to end racial discrimination for the good of society. It was not intended as a permanent solution but rather as temporary until such time that people of color could overcome fears that they would be considered to be inferior or judged unfairly. As decreed by law, discrimination in five categories—of race, color, gender, religion, and national origin—was henceforth illegal (Davidson and Anderson, 1982).

People's perception of Affirmative Action today differs significantly from its original function as set out in the Wagner Act. This new instantiation of Affirmative Action was first challenged in the landmark decision of the *Regents of the University of California v. Bakke* (Jacobson, 1983). In California, a three-judge panel of the U.S. Court of Appeals for the Fifth Circuit undercut the state Supreme Court's decision regarding the 1978 Bakke case by finding Affirmative Action programs to be illegal (O'Neille, 1985). In another case, the state of Texas suspended several scholarship programs for minority students. Its law school was barred from using racial preferences for admissions or awarding financial aid to needy blacks and Latinos. Critics insist their efforts are not intended to harm African people but rather to ensure that others are not discriminated against in the process. Barring whatever one's position is on Affirmative Action today, few if any objections were raised when it was applied to the benefit of white males. The fact that African Americans cannot be accorded equal access is a blatant example of the conservative political agenda that, since the antebellum, has sought to exploit all institutions of society in the interest of the white population. Given the aforementioned, facts merit a psychological explanation of blacks that would support a conservative political agenda dedicated to sustaining the oppression of the African people.

The white power structure, comprised of old white Anglo-Saxon protestant families and their friends, exercises more authority in America than their numbers would suggest. Relative to authority within economic, social, and political institutions, whites exercise power, whereas the majority of blacks, particularly those who remain under oppressive situations of health, work, and welfare, are the objects of whites' acts of power.

Robert F. Bales is recognized as one of the major American political scientists in the twentieth century, and he claimed that within the act of enacting power, there exists two primary forms of authority (1951). The first is authority as an instrumental form, in which subjects are required to assist to achieve some group goal. The second occurs when group unity and harmony is reinforced relative to in-group membership. To be effective in promoting a conservative political agenda, both instrumental and group unity forms are necessary, and this is especially true among African conservatives, who are willing to facilitate African oppression in spite of being black (Bales, 1951, pp. 89–132).

Thus, the two primary functions of authority are often utilized against those who do not have power, whether it be a child in a family or Africans or Latinos in certain societies. Bales (1951) explained the existence of such authority relations by appealing to the division of roles evident within the traditional Western nuclear family unit. Here, the patriarch exercises instrumental authority, whereas the matriarch provides group unity via warmth, comfort, and so forth. Evidence of this practice among African conservatives, in which the white power structure is both master and father, establishes the relevancy of this theory when analyzing the conservative political agenda.

In addition to its different manifestations, authority can be realized through a variety of methods. In their classic mid-twentieth-century work,

Lewin, Lippit, and White (1939) investigated authority as domination associated with leadership. They exposed youths to three forms of leadership: authoritarian, democratic, and laissez-faire. They then observed the impact of these different leadership styles on the subjects' behavior. The results revealed a number of differences between the effects of the different styles. Under the authoritarian style, the leader was the sole determinant of group activity, such as policy and the designation of specific tasks. Under the democratic style, policy and specific tasks were determined by group discussion, in which the leader participated. Lastly, under the laissez-faire style, the subjects were in complete control, assisted by very minimal input from the leader. What is more, the way in which leaders praised and criticized the youthful male subjects differed by style as well. In reference to authoritarian leaders, group criticisms were made personal. Those exposed to democratic leaders experienced an environment of fairness and objectivity. In contrast, in the laissez-faire group, leaders commented little and otherwise left group regulation totally to the subject male youth.

In the aftermath of these differing leadership styles, according to Shaw (1976), subjects experienced 30 times more hostility in the authoritarian group than in the democratic group, including 8 times more aggression. Additionally, under authoritarian leadership, subjects took part in significant levels of scapegoating, in which others were assigned blame similar to that found in racism, sexism, and so forth. Those exposed to democratic leaders appreciated their leaders more than those exposed to authoritarian leaders, being preferred over the other by 19 of the 20 subjects. Additionally, 7 out of 10 boys preferred the laissez-faire leaders to the authoritarian style. Although there was no appreciable difference in quantity of productivity between styles, the products of the democratic leadership style appeared to be of better quality than of other groups. Likewise, in contrast to conservative claims, liberal politics is more commensurate with the democratic leadership style. African Americans are typically more liberal than conservative primarily because the style of liberal philosophy and leadership agrees with the general idea of progressive social interactions.

Furthermore, the manner in which leaders emerge from the membership was studied by George C. Homans (1974), who stated that group leaders are generally those who manifest something unique and are accorded a special status by group members. In addition, other investigators contend that leaders consist of persons who play a major role in the activities of the group (Crosbie, 1975). Subsequently, leaders may be predisposed to lead and followers to follow. Thus, the most critical element of group behavior comes down to the question of being person-centered versus having circumstances requiring action. We can understand how this problematizes the situation with the spiritual descendants of the house Negroes, who are often seen as or looked to by white conservatives to be the leaders of the black people, but in reality they have no credibility with the majority of blacks.

Following World War II, sociologists at the University of California-Berkeley investigated the notion of a person-centered hypothesis to determine its significance in leadership styles. They concluded that there is a specific personality type that is predisposed to rigidity and group hierarchical authority, hence the authoritarian personality. The essence of their psychology is commensurate with the house Negro African conservative, whose underlying desire is to please the all-powerful authoritarian white father vis-à-vis white power structure. The result is an African person inclined to blind obedience and submission to a conservative political agenda despite its implications for African folk (Adorno, Frenkel-Brunswik, Levinson, and Sanford, 1950).

To illustrate this point, investigators gathered empirical evidence from American respondents using clinical interviews and attitude tests. They consistently found the tendency toward obedience in some respondents, which they again defined as authoritarian personalities. Relative to the African people, authoritarian personalities are prone to prejudice and also maintain specific sentiments regarding how authority should be treated and maintained, including submission to those in power, harshness to those regarded as powerless, and a pronounced belief in the significance of power and the domination of others. The authoritarian personality consistently agrees with such statements on the attitude scales as, "Obedience and respect for authority are the most important virtues children should learn"; "Most of our social problems would be solved if we could somehow get rid of the immoral, the crooked and feeble-minded people"; and "People can be divided into two distinct classes: the weak and the strong" (Adorno, Frenkel-Brunswik, Levinson, and Sanford, 1950, p. 50).

Researchers at the University of California at Berkeley further contend that this psychological pattern is a demonstration of subliminal personality traits that African conservatives may have formed during their childhood. Subsequently, test subjects who scored high on minority prejudice and authoritarianism also depicted their childhoods as being dominated by a rigid, all-powerful father figure who demanded absolute obedience. In a Freudianesque manner, children dominated to such an extent have few options other than to suppress or negate any hostility toward their power-superior father. They cannot afford even to merely acknowledge such hostility because to do so would force it out of the subconscious. They develop what psychoanalysts term a "reaction formation" (Gleitman, 1986, p. 112). That is, as the powerless victims of their all-powerful father's domination, they adopt the inverse response by becoming totally obedient as a matter of justifiable virtue. However, their hostile feelings are not diminished completely but instead are redirected at less formidable victims, including racial minorities, which, for African conservatives, involves other blacks or members of other less powerful groups. To sustain this redirection of hostility, they place high value on "toughness" and an equally valued taboo on weakness. Thus, these respondents redirected toward others the hostility that they could not acknowledge in themselves.

Similar to African conservatives who fault African Americans solely for social and racial problems, there is evidence of another defense mechanism used by African conservatives called "projection." In projection, the ego expels any personal attributes it cannot assimilate into its ideal personality structure (Gleitman, 1986). Using such logic, any nonconservative is perceived by the African conservative as inferior and as being among the hordes of destructive barbarians who would annihilate peaceful and/or weaker populations if given the chance. Thus, in conservative parlance, Latinos, Asians, Jews, foreigners, religious aliens, and the masses of underclass blacks require control by subjecting them to the power of conservative political authority and, if necessary—especially during the antebellum—violence.

Relative to principles of the authoritarian conservative political agenda, classical definitions of authoritarianism emphasize the rejection of Africans, which, for black conservatives, means self-rejection. In a predominantly white Judeo-Christian group, the black conservatives may be a small minority (Kitano, 1985), but they represent the philosophically and socially rejected group. They are like the victims of oppression in any society who gravitate toward those who are the persecutors of their own people. This was the case with the D'Souzas in the old Dahomey kingdom. The children of the Portuguese slave trader, the D'Souzas, became, for all practical purposes, slave traders themselves who sold their mothers' children to other slave traders. But this is an extreme example. In another instance, women in some oppressive religious communities become the very ones who carry out the surveillance and abuse of other women in the name of protecting the social structure. We have seen this in Afghanistan, Pakistan, Iraq, and Iran in recent years.

A particularly virulent form of conservative group psychology has come to insist on absolute devotion to the conservative political agenda in response to what it perceives as anti-Americanism. This reaction further helps the conservative political agenda, in which the oppression of Africans is not only ignored but actually may be an integral part of political strategy. As a result, African conservatives are convinced that toleration of African oppression is justified in order to realize their authoritarian political agenda. This is, in effect, the house Negro seeking to ensure the survival of the plantation by reporting rumors of slave revolts as a way to advance the white supremacist agenda.

In an effort to maintain itself, the African conservative authoritarian personality necessarily sublimates any tendencies and/or impulses it perceives as racially unacceptable. Thus, they must eliminate from consciousness any matter identifying them with the mass underclass, which is what occurred among house Negroes during the antebellum. Relaxing their rigidity will threaten to compromise defenses, which would result in a breakthrough of despised sublimated tendencies. Even when sublimated too rigorously or too soon in life, these despised tendencies do not lose their potency. Conversely, immediate or failed sublimation inhibits rather than assists in the process of rigidity and sublimation (Adorno, Frenkel-Brunswik, Levinson, and Sanford, 1950). Under the circumstances, a healthy ego that is compromised will be confronted with the possibility of becoming completely besieged by sublimated influences. Increased rigidity of defense mechanisms will enable African conservatives to tolerate the increased threat posed by their membership in the African community. Despite such rigidity, sublimated influences do manage to escape from their control. Intense instinctual impulses are constantly taxing their egos to the extent that they must be forever vigilant. Legitimate control occupies a limited domain of their personality, severely distorting its appropriate application. Thus, as long as control and domination exceed other conditions and as long as the conservative political agenda makes permissible portals for sublimated impulses available, societal functioning—however limited—can be realized. It is through this authoritarian psychology that African conservatives enable African oppression via the conservative political agenda (D'Souza, 1991).

Modern-day conservative political agendas are not acted out by disgruntled individuals working alone; instead, they are most likely the collective responsibilities of groups of like-minded people working to bring into existence a conservative phalanx against what they view as an aggressive progressivism (Walter, 1969). Seldom are random acts of African oppression carried out without careful planning and deliberate outcomes because these acts are products of political objectives. What would appear to be actions directed at the African people are, in fact, the aftermath of conservative political operatives whose authoritarian dictates define negotiated compromise as defeat. They aim to control and dominate African folk, whom they perceive as inferior. For the African conservative, this ultimately justifies any actions necessary for desired political outcome. They do not act alone but instead act in concert with their white power structure father figure (Kitano, 1985). However, the formidable influence of conservative rhetoric has all but ignored the psychology of the African conservative in a way that sanitizes African oppression as being motivated by the same inferior tendencies assumed of the inferior antebellum field Negroes. Fortunately, the actions of African conservatives have spurred serious discourse in an effort to understand the impact of oppression on individuals. One such discussion pertains to J. H. Duckitt's (1989) analysis of authoritarianism.

Duckitt believed that African oppression is not solely a matter of intent to do harm but rather is more likely an authoritarian identification with an exclusive white power structure whose objective is to control and/or dominate the African people, which it defines as a threatening out-group. Currently, the psychology of the in-group versus out-group dynamics in a political context sustains the conservative political agenda. In-group versus out-group differentiations in political contexts include alien races, alien norms, alien beliefs, and any other alien factor, including what might otherwise be regarded as trivial absent conservative sentiments (Kitano, 1985). This concept is not new, but was in fact suggested by Gordon Allport (1954) in his study of understanding the nature of prejudice. The study of prejudice is relevant to Henri Tajfel's (1981) work on group attachment theory. The theoretical significance of these scientists' work is grounded in empirical evidence and context provided by Allport's earlier findings; thus, one sees this connection, notably in the work of L. L. Downing and N. R. Monaco (1986). After conducting various field experiments, they concluded that in-group authoritarian conservative personalities are particularly prone to oppression. Furthermore, in a report of their findings, Horowitz and Rabbie (1982) noted more extensive authoritarian personalities among males compared to females:

> The pattern of these findings resembles that reported by Downing and Monaco ... for authoritarians and non-authoritarians. One might say that, like authoritarians, males are relatively predisposed to perceive aggregates of individuals as groups; conversely, that females, like non-authoritarians, are predisposed to perceive aggregates of individuals as separate persons. Being disposed to view others as members, males rate in-group members higher than out-group members.

The aforementioned research illuminates the extent of pathology associated with the African conservatives and their political agenda. Despite this, conservative operatives continue to direct blame for African oppression on African behavior under African control (Adorno, Frenkel-Brunswik, Levinson, and Sanford, 1950). Because Western civilization has much greater longevity and power to control those it deems as inferior, those who are so labeled have become the stereotypical focus of oppression. This encourages a hostile political environment that polarizes various group factions that might otherwise be amenable to negotiated compromise conducive to peaceful coexistence.

African conservatives who are willing to delude other African Americans for pay in the interest of white conservative political interests are not limited to media pundits who peddle public policies. Political operatives reach into the most esteemed halls of academia and, by way of political agenda, manipulate some of the most intellectually gifted among African scholars in America today. These scholars are skilled and aristocratic in every sense. Their political perspectives are seldom challenged, given their prestigious educations and host institutions. In values, norms, and lifestyle, they demonstrate the aristocratic house Negro elite. One such scholar, Thomas Sowell, is currently a professor at Stanford University, and his most recent work is titled *Black Rednecks and White Liberals* (2005). As a matter of public debate, his conservative interpretation of historical events is, if nothing else, worthy of consideration for its unique point of view. By tracing the cultural norms of African Americans to England's "redneck" population, this Harvard-educated conservative African scholar provides an interesting alternative to the origin of Western civilization's social ills, which he attributes to the masses of lower socioeconomic blacks—that is, field Negroes. His disdain for the African community is similar to that of antebellum–era house Negroes who advocated for a three-tiered Louisiana class system that would make them separate and distinct from the African people whom they despised (Gatewood, 2000). In reading Sowell's work, we find a pattern of discrepancies of factual accuracy.

After reviewing *African Rednecks and White Liberals*, we find that Sowell tends to omit single words from quoted material or certain facts from historic narratives that change the meaning of the text; given his skill and intellectual talent, we cannot attribute this to error because it is actually a consistent pattern of black conservative scholarship. For example, *Webster's* dictionary defines the word "quote" as "to give exact information on," set off by quotation marks. On page 230 of *African Rednecks and White Liberals*, Sowell quotes from *An American Dilemma* (Myrdal, 1944): "High schools for Negroes in the South have existed in significant numbers for only about twenty years and are still inadequate." According to the original source, the quote, found on page 950, was stated incorrectly in the citation. The words are the same, but there is also a footnote after the word "years" that states that although there were only 64 public schools for blacks, there were also 216 private schools. Thus, without empirical evidence, the whole of African education is dismissed as inadequate—a conservative aristocratic observation. If a quotation requires an exact reference, an objective scholar would not have excluded the footnote. Ideally, it would have been acknowledged and then an explanation would have been offered.

In a similar distortion of facts, on page 256, Sowell discusses Frazier's *Black Bourgeoisie* (1957): "Frazier commented on how seldom even African college faculty read books." Returning to the source, Frazier actually proposed, as written on page 74, that "many of the teachers of English and literature never read a book as a source of pleasure or recreation." Although African faculties personally may have read 15 to 20 books per year, a significant number seldom read a book for pleasure. Reading for pleasure is distinct from not reading at all, which is what the African conservative author suggests.

In a more subtle misstatement, the author again leads readers to unsubstantiated characterizations of prominent African historical figures and the celebration of white college educational systems by describing African colleges as inferior in every way rather than discussing their weaknesses as imitations of white institutions. He cites one instance of W. E. B. Du Bois having paid tribute to the aristocratic house negro Booker T. Washington. Sowell argues that liberals and African civil rights activists had misrepresented the amicable relationship between the men. Sowell stated that in 1905 DuBois secretly met with a group of African activists in New York to "renounce Booker T. Washington's accommodation policies set forth in his famed Atlanta Compromise" (Sowell, 2005, p. 138). In fact, however, the whole of DuBois's life and work had been devoted to opposing Washington and all that he espoused. This is not to say that they did not cooperate on a few initiatives, such as the book they wrote together, but, overall, DuBois had sharp intellectual differences with Washington.

Then, in the same instance, Sowell contradicts himself when he denounces African American colleges by referencing African college intellectuals such as DuBois, who, in fact, was one of the most important academics in American history. No doubt some who were teaching at African colleges may have been less qualified than their white counterparts, but those who were exceptionally qualified at both the high school and black college level balanced the faculty quality. They included DuBois himself, who graduated from Fisk—an African college—and became the first African American to earn a PhD from Harvard (McKissick and McKissick, 1990). Booker T. Washington was also educated at Hampton Institute before he founded another African college, Tuskegee Institute (Andrews, 1996). Another was E. Franklin Frazier, whom the author also quotes frequently. The first African to sit on the U.S. Supreme Court of the United States, Justice Thurgood Marshall, was an African college graduate who had been rejected by the University of Maryland Law School (Smith, 2001). Charles Drew benefited Western medicine with his gifts to blood plasma technology (Richardson, 1945). What the giants have in common is that they either graduated from an African college, were faculty members, or both.

Thus, although Sowell names Atlanta University specifically as one of the inferior African institutions of the day, he fails to acknowledge that DuBois, E. Franklin Frazier, and other prominent African intellectuals had taught there for years. In fact, African colleges have produced some of the most prominent African Americans to date, alumnae who are conservative as well as liberal, including Armstrong Williams from South Carolina State and Martin Luther King, Jr., from Morehouse College (Kirk, 2005). Although Sowell references to African education are not inaccurate facts, the particular facts he chooses to present leave the unknowing reader with a grossly distorted view of the entirety of African education. Ultimately, such a view facilitates the control of education by white institutions that, as a conservative political agenda, are not amenable to the education of African students.

The most obvious commonality between the existence of antebellum house Negroes and modern-day African conservatives is their accommodation of the conservative political agenda. In the aftermath, African conservatives, such as Ward Connerly, abhor programs like Affirmative Action despite its benefits to the African community because, as per the conservative political agenda, it is an affront to the master class. A pattern of such abhorrence by African conservatives sustains quality of life differentials between African and white Americans. Subsequently, whites continue to exceed blacks in every quality of life category, including education, occupation, income, housing, power, and status (Kitano, 1985). Blacks' relative inferior statistics in each category are made possible by some degree of political submission by the few blacks who have benefited. Consequently, their submission encourages African conservatives to negotiate with a hostile political element with which they have no bargaining power. Their role is to serve as political gatekeepers in order to adopt conservative policies that are otherwise destructive to the viability of the African community as a whole.

Conservatism, as defined by Agre, cannot be tolerated in the context of an evolving democracy (2004). The masses of African people remain among the most oppressed in the modern world, but that oppression has not been such as to eliminate optimism (Hall, 2003). The tenacious struggle against oppression has sustained a measurable degree of hope. A few among African conservatives have been inspired by the strength and courage of the masses, prompting them—unlike antebellum house Negroes—to celebrate their blackness (Steins, 2003). Indeed, a few who have served conservative interests, such as Colin Powell, have not only embraced their blackness but acknowledged the conservative links to the oppression of African people as a whole despite the implications for them politically and their personal quality of life. Their most daunting task will be to invest their talents to devise a strategy to politically, economically, and socially rescue the masses from the oppression of conservatism that, in America, has become all but institutionalized in the modern era (Akbar, 2004).

One of the most effective strategies to reverse the process and rescue the masses of African folk from the conservative political agenda is to utilize self-affirming institutions (Akbar, 2004). Rituals, literature, and memorials are a few such examples that will attend to the pathologies of oppression in order to persuade African conservatives to work for the welfare of their group. Enslaved Africans, having been disconnected from traditional sources of self-affirmation, were grist for the evolution of house Negroes. Asante (2003) suggested a plausible strategy for rescuing African conservatives and the masses of African folk from the political forces of conservatism in the modern era. These strategies, according to Asante, are immediate possibilities for most American communities. Without a historical base for action, Africans are not able to develop a social consciousness that will eliminate intellectual dependence on the slave master's narrative. Indeed, as Asante understood, consciousness is not achieved on the terms of those who intend to maintain their power over you; instead, knowledge of history and self is the key to personal transformation. Like Ama Mazama, the Afrocentric theorist, Asante claims that the lack of transformation found in black communities throughout the world derives from the lack of historical and social consciousness (Mazama, 2003). People do what they know how to do, and most do not know how to save themselves from the numbing consistency of oppressive institutions because they continue to look to those very institutions for salvation. Like the house Negro seeking liberation from the slave master, in reality, that salvation will only come when he realizes, through hearsay, experience, example, or other forms of knowledge, that there is no right that gives the slave holder the authority to hold the African in bondage. Such knowledge marks the beginning of the consciousness of self-delivery—that is, self-liberation.

The atrocities faced by African Americans during the antebellum era have often been omitted from serious public discourse. But this particular omission is not a unique case. We know little about the persecution of the Africans in Colombia, Brazil, Uruguay, Ecuador, Peru, Jamaica, and so forth, mainly because the white power structures do not consider worthy of preservation the narratives of the enslaved, like that of the colonized during the Algerian occupation by France or the British occupation of Zimbabwe, Ghana, and Nigeria. However, when consciousness captures the imagination of the oppressed, then it will also impress the descendants of the oppressors. When President Clinton proposed formally apologizing to African Americans for slavery, he drew an unprecedented amount of anger from conservatives in the United States, as if this mere suggestion surpassed the brutalities of the crime (Torpey, 2006). This response was purely a matter of politics that flew in the face of universal ethics. However, in order to heal past wounds, America must embrace the totality of its history, including its racist oppression of Africans. This will give license to scholars and academics to rewrite this nation's story from a more global and factually accurate perspective. Unfortunately, it is not possible to forget the past, as President Barack Obama encouraged the leaders of Africa to do when he visited Accra, Ghana, in July 2009. Obama implored Africans to close the book on citing colonization as a reason that Africa has been slow to progress. However, neither Africa nor America can close that book just yet. The ability to embrace the past will enable this nation to operate in a present arena capable of addressing necessary courses of action, which might then be made operational without respect to conservative or other political agendas. Thus, what occurred during the American antebellum era would not be limited to the victimization of African people but, like the holocaust, would be regarded as an atrocity against humankind (Mazama 2003, pp. 3–12). In that context, American society will begin to validate the cultural rights of every ethnic group as worthy of universal respect and dignity. Our ability to incorporate the aforementioned strategies will help us embrace this nation's history, and doing so will then make it possible to discuss reparations for slavery as a fair and just consideration.

Lastly, democratic ideals, as central to the future of African people in America, help to define and determine African Americans' reality. The African conservative's role in the conservative political agenda should not be dismissed as irrelevant to the welfare of African people but rather should be investigated so as to decode convoluted research, illuminate class hierarchy, and, if necessary, move to political action. In many ways, the work of the black conservatives has been ahistorical in the sense that they have been careless with the historical facts and the political currents in American society. Their legacies have not been without precedent but, in fact, exist as a continuum wedded to the larger construction of a fragmented African

American intelligentsia. Neither African nor white conservatives in America understand or accept the role of advocacy for African interests. One could hope—indeed wish—black conservatives could transcend selfish interests, personal gain, and political residence in the master's house in order to make a significant contribution to the civil evolution of the nation. Perhaps, if there is a Barack Obama era, black conservatives may find their voices through helping to develop of a new approach to the American agenda.

# CHAPTER FIVE

# Self-Mutilation in the Master's House

The death of popular music star Michael Jackson in July 2009 unleashed, inter alia, a torrent of discourse about his physical change in color from the time when he was young to adulthood. For weeks, television programs showed how he transformed from a beautiful cocoa-complexioned teenager to a bizarre whiter-than-white adult with an altered facial structure. The question was, "Did Michael Jackson hate being black or was he trying to transcend race?" Whatever else one concludes about Jackson based on the evidence, it now seems clear that he sought to escape the natural condition of his skin and facial structure. We cannot say that he hated being black but rather that he wanted to escape his condition. We recognize that this is a nuanced and sensitive issue, so we will try to explain what we mean. There is no question that Jackson did not want to be seen in the skin that he had. Thus, the question remains whether this would have been the case if his skin had been white? Some who were acquainted with Jackson believe that he wanted to make himself unrecognizable, to distort the image that people had of him as a superstar, to mangle the icon and to twist it into something that might even be unlovable. If this is the case, ironically, in transforming his physical being, he made himself more visible, more iconic, and, indeed, in the opinion of some, less human.

Although Jackson's musical genius was undisputed and his naturally gifted rhythmic African moves sent millions to buy his DVDs, his enigmatic personality and the unnatural whitening of his skin, whether because of vitiligo or not, sparked a discourse around his obsession with skin color. Furthermore, he could not transcend race because he chose to become white and, in America, white was still a racial classification. He did not seek to be purple, for example. Thus, when Jackson transformed his skin color, he unwittingly brought to light something that we have always known in the black American community and, indeed, increasingly in the African community: some blacks despise their own skin color and use every kind of bleaching product available to distance themselves from the color they associate with slavery and colonization. They think, in their confusion, that oppression occurred historically because they were black and that divinity must have chosen whiteness to rule over them. They believe, therefore, that white is better and more beautiful than black, so they will do anything to achieve the status of whiteness.

Self-mutilation of blackness occurred first among the house Negroes, who had access to the master's most intimate secrets. The blacks who worked in the house prepared the oils, soaps, and creams used by the mistress as she beautified herself. They were the first blacks to be enamored with the whiteness of the skin of the master's family. They believed that there was a magic to whiteness, that is, in a religious sense: As they were reminded, the Christian god had graced the white people with skin that was pure whereas black people were given impure complexion, a blackness that represented all forms of sin and evil. With such overwhelming evidence as the power that whites exercised over blacks, what would possess a human being to want to be black? But what if one could not help the skin he or she was born with? The house Negro begins to think, with a vengeance, about self-mutilation: You could try to change the color of your skin and perhaps change the texture of your hair. Black people pursued these objectives as the initial steps into an entire catalogue of insanity.

In the aftermath of the antebellum period, Africans in the United States experienced an institutionalized form of image destruction that assaulted the color and the features of Africans. We were made to appear grotesque in books, magazines, and later in movies such as *The Birth of a Nation*. This attack on blackness, along with our relative poverty and impotence as a people, translated into black self-hatred. People sought to straighten their hair, lighten their skin, and do anything that might diminish blackness.

Some Africans tried to use any type of bleaching element in their efforts to reach what they perceived as the white American ideal (Hall, 2006, pp. 19–31). If someone was bleaching his or her skin, the surrounding community considered this unmentionable yet something that was understood by all. By internalizing the destructive images against blackness with no other images coming into one's consciousness to counteract those images, blacks became unshakably dependent on the belief in the negativity of blackness. Light-skinned blacks who had white ancestry, more often than not received favors from the white authorities. This practice furthered the self-hatred darker-skinned persons experienced. What's more, this is not simply an American problem; it is profoundly the condition of the African in every country in the Americas as well as in many places on the continent of Africa itself. Black self-mutilation to change the natural appearance of skin and hair became one of the dominant and persistent patterns of black life after the turn of the twentieth century, but we can find the origins of the confusion and self-mutilation in the master's house. It was the incubator for the most horrific examples of black self-mutilation when the house Negroes would use the white mistress's dressing rooms, in her absence, and feign that they were the mistresses of the house, or the glee male house Negroes felt when they would try on the master's shoes and sporting coats while the master was out of town. Of course, if the enslaved person were caught, his sentence would be an immediate 40 lashes of the whip across a bare back. The coat, shoes, or dresses used in the self-satisfying imitation of the whites would have to be thrown away because a white person could never wear what a black person had worn—perhaps the black skin of the black person had stained the clothes or had been shed in the shoes. The problem of skin color posed a special situation for Africans trying to emerge from under the yoke of bondage.

Imposing a skin color ideal—that is, thrusting light skin onto the psyche of the African—is extensive, extending to contemporary relationships, in which white images are unyielding and tenacious throughout all forms of media. Without exception, the white or, if not white, certainly light skin color ideal is an environmental social force that disrupts the psychological well-being of Africans, resulting in the bleaching syndrome.

Indeed, the bleaching syndrome is similar to the dramatic acting out of conservative tendencies, in which black people imitate white people. Such people often view any form of African acceptance as negative, thus ensuring that the modern-day cultural self-hatred ideal is perpetuated. The bleaching syndrome is a product of African self-hate being dramatically acted out politically by the modern-day African conservative (Hall,

2006, pp. 19–30). Although the literature acknowledges the widespread existence of destructive African images, its political implications have been largely ignored amidst the Eurocentric bias of scholarly literature. But this phenomenon is not unattached from the conservative ideas advanced by certain blacks. For example, John McWhorter, Senior Fellow at the conservative Manhattan Institute, in his article "What Black Studies Can Do," claimed that some Black Studies departments believe that "In 'conservative' black thought, coherence, morality and feasibility are so utterly implausible that they do not merit consideration as meaningful information to impart to young minds" (2009, July 15). This is a prime example of a black conservative failing to see how the house Negro syndrome has extended into intellectual thought. Indeed, McWhorter has insisted that Black Studies, a discipline born of struggle against illiberal and reactionary thought, should raise black conservative thinkers such as Stanley Crouch, Debra Dickerson, and Shelby Steele—people who are opposed to Black Studies—to the level of serious discussion. Why would progressive Jewish Studies seriously consider raising to high discourse those Jews who are holocaust deniers? When black writers turn against their own traditions simply for aggrandizement, can this ever be praised or raised? It must be criticized as deceitful and, perhaps, even sinister.

One can ask similar questions about people who live as blacks in their careers but then feel they must assert that they are "half Irish" or "half English." This is similar to the urge to bleach the skin because blackness is only biological in a small way; it is profoundly much more about perception, hopes, visions, and possibilities. Those blacks who believe that bleaching is essential for gaining access to white privilege are no less irrational than those black conservatives who believe that, by bashing Black Studies, they demonstrate their conservative mettle and, hence, ensure recognition by the white master. This was the role played by individuals such as Armstrong Williams, Anne Wortham, Shelby Steele, Thomas Sowell, and Dinesh D'Souza, each in his or her own way at certain times over the past 25 years. What they all share is a decidedly antagonistic bent toward Africans who work for the interest of black freedom, liberation, escape from mental slavery, and collective economic and social elevation. In fact, such black conservatives are more likely than not to also believe that white is better in everything and at everything, and they would state that black students and black people should follow the paths of whites, even if it means changing or distorting their color and image in order to make themselves present-able to whites.

Bleaching the skin is not merely a physical act; it is profoundly a psychological choice. Of all the manifestations of the bleaching syndrome, the physical aspect of race is, without a doubt, the least important. Given politics, geography, and economics, gene pools will alter race over time. Who African people are in the United States today is not necessarily who we will be tomorrow because that is based solely on the strength of African identity. The world is nothing more than a history of the changing gene pools of humanity. Now the implications of change, modification, and difference are numerous and must include the black conservatives' search for bleaching creams to alter their appearances and color. We should be clear here that this is not a problem found only among African Americans; it is also found among Asians, Mexicans, and Indians who have been in contact with the white Western world (see, for example, www.youtube.com/watch?v=F-9tcXpW1DE and www.cnn.com/2009/WORLD/asiapcf/09/09/india.skin/index.html). There is a psychological component to this phenomenon as it seems to occur where people have lost the possession of their traditional ancestral values or are in search of social, economic, or cultural privileges that appear to accompany white skin.

Undoubtedly, the event that had the single most important impact on the black consciousness was the social and cultural movement that accompanied the political and economic arguments of the 1960s. Reducing psychological self-hatred was a by-product of the campaign for empowerment. During the most intense period of the "Black is Beautiful" campaign, no one dared express sentiment for skin bleaching. If anything, black people wanted to be black. However, this movement was shut down by the rise of Reagan conservatives, who oversaw new possibilities being slowly killed and "identity politics" maligned. Although this transformative movement had inspired Latinos, Native Americans, and Asians, its primary purpose was to raise black people from historical slumber. By the 1970s, as more African people became political activists, we began to realize just how firm and far-reaching the psychological self-hate seemed to be among us. Some became pessimistic and disillusioned about the prospect of overcoming such formidable obstacles inherited from the plantation.

There were not only Africans who expressed a dislike for their own skin color because of the racializing of color, but there were also others who thought that their hair was bad because it was not straight like the whites who were the economic masters of society. These blacks engaged in a tradition of abnormal hairstyling that went back to the plantation. When house Negroes, as young girls, were charged with combing the hair of their mistresses for hours upon hours, they developed an appreciation for white women's hair that simultaneously resulted in devaluing their own hair. The white person's hair had two traits that were especially appealing to the young house Negroes charged with keeping the white mistresses of the house groomed. First, it was straight, and second, it was much easier to comb than black hair. No historians or sociologists or plantation elders could explain this difference through geographical origin, biology, climate, or adaptability; the only thing the house Negro could see was that the white woman's hair was different than hers. Furthermore, the whites were not just different; they were more powerful, richer, and property owners, whereas the Africans were weak and powerless.

It is no wonder that some of the house Negroes took to using the cloth iron to press their hair whenever the plantation owners were out of the house, experimenting with it by having one woman lay her head to the side on the kitchen table while another placed the hot iron on her bushy hair. The result was dramatic: The heat tore through the kinks and straightened the hair! Hallelujah! Later they would add oils—mostly animal oils, but also fish oils—to the process. It was painful, could be extremely dangerous, and often caused sores on the head. However, the suffering was considered a part of the process of overcoming the natural kinkiness in order to achieve the holiness of straight hair. Wearing scarves to hide the attempt at straightening their kinks created a form of subterfuge, mystery, and curiosity. This was a specialized process reserved only for the house Negroes who were close to the whites and could make use of the whites' irons at will, or at least when they had a moment's leisure. The field Negroes had no such luck. They were stuck with the kinky hair until a process they could access could be developed that would reduce the difficulty and danger.

Madame C. J. Walker, who was born to former slaves as Sarah Breedlove, became the first black millionaire because of her inventions for black hair. Although the hot comb was the principal element in her technique, she also invented various hair softeners for black hair. By the end of the nineteenth and turn of the twentieth century, Madame Walker had become the most prominent promoter of black hair products. None of these products were designed to elevate the kinky hair style; instead, all of them were meant to make the black woman's hair appear more like the white woman's. Thus, in many ways the Afro hairstyle of the 1960s was the most revolutionary act of the Black is Beautiful era because it rejected the straightening regime. Nevertheless, self-hatred continued to rob the African American community of its greatest strength: its own initiative and agency.

However, alliances and coalitions of progressive and sympathetic whites, together with blacks and browns, created a unified multicultural front that supported social, cultural, and psychological well-being. Nothing like this had occurred since the 1950s, when the Civil Rights Movement mobilized thousands of blacks and whites to confront racism and segregation. Now, in the movements of the late 1960s and early 1970s, blacks and whites with raised consciousness again united against war, distortion, lies, and unreality in areas of skin color bleaching and they advocated for authenticity. We created an equally formidable force to confront the colonial and antebellum residue, not only in terms of hard-core political abuse but also psychologically damaging images of black people. This movement polarized the nation. There were some people who agreed with the movement and some who were against it, but those of us at the vanguard had to wage the struggle for cultural and political liberation wholeheartedly and without reservation. Maulana Karenga, the charismatic leader of the Us Organization, was one of the first to say that the issue confronting the black community was one of "culture." The idea that culture was the root of our problem in the African American community challenged a segment of the movement; indeed, it split the movement—with the Black Panthers advocating revolutionary nationalism and the Karenga followers arguing we needed to create a culture for revolution before we could bring about a revolution. There was no revolutionary culture among black people, although the black community produced many speeches, articles, and pamphlets in order to bring about revolution in our lifetimes. The cultural nationalists, as they were called, sought an assault on the negativity that surrounded blackness. Because of this, the movement took exception to skin bleaching. Doing so was seen as a physical example of self-hatred and a contemporary manifestation of the house Negro syndrome. It clearly indicated in precise terms that racism had created far more damage than simply segregating us physically or working us nearly to death on the plantation. Racism had demonstrated that its tentacles could reach into every African American home to create havoc.

Racism remains the most destructively dramatic American social construct, yet black conservatives have found it less relevant to their politics (B. F. Jones, 1966, pp. 106–130). The fact that the African conservative considers racism less relevant demonstrates the extent of the psychological damage he has not only endured but actually embraced. In fact, the social connotation of the destructive African image exacerbates the impact that these alien ideals have on his psyche. Consequently, African conservatives continue to distance themselves from the African community whenever possible. We see this in the essay referenced earlier by John McWhorter. He discovers, with a bit of glee, what he considers to be another way to take on black students' historical struggle against racist curricula, and he does so by distancing himself from the relevancy of the movement with a tongue-in-cheek essay. But one thing is perfectly clear: the African community cannot remain viable if a significant element within the population continues to submit itself to ideals of self-destruction and self-hatred (Gitterman, 1991, p. 21). Hence, in the current era, it is imperative that we examine the legacy of enslavement and discrimination for its psychological impact on African people. Only then will it be possible to separate ideology from ontology in the discourse of black conservatives.

The issue of skin color unfortunately remains with us in American society. It has affected blacks in a negative manner, and there are still those who believe that light skin is preferable in all matters of life and public affairs. Whites' vilification of dark skin carries implications for personal choice in mates as well, where darker-complexioned African Americans seek out lighter-complexioned ones to marry. However, there are exceptions to this, as we know that some lighter-complexioned blacks choose darker-skinned blacks in order to make their own statement about attachment to African history and culture.

During the Black Power Era of the 1960s, black skin color was considered a part of the ideological battle being fought by blacks. The popular mass movement made it unacceptable to think less of dark skin. African Americans in the movement valued their blackness and saw it as beautiful. A locally fashioned brand of self-love was embraced by the masses, and "Black is beautiful" was the ethnic motto. Such activism encouraged large numbers of African Americans to stop straightening their hair. To prefer natural hair was to make one of the most revolutionary statements of the era. Indeed, women and men wore their Afros proudly and deflated the hair care industry by searching for natural oils and traditional methods of hair care. Today, although men remained essentially committed to African hair styles, black women have found it much more difficult to remain consistent. Thus, during the beginning of the twenty-first century, many black women have resumed straightening their hair and using hair extensions.

During the enslavement, white skin and the white race were the overwhelming dominant categories of preferred social status. However, sexual liaisons between slave masters and black women produced large numbers of light-complexioned Africans. These people were often referred to as mulattos, octoroons, or people of color. There were also limited cases of black men and white women in the North producing children that also became identified with this social class. Even though these relationships occurred, it was not until the legal case of *Loving v. the State of Virginia* that all vestiges of the prohibition of interracial marriage were outlawed (Virginia Law Review, 1966, pp. 1189–1223).

Skin color remains, even now, a part of the American catalogue of manipulated traits in social narratives. Today, the use of electronic photographic images has shown the impact of darkening or lightening images to provoke either negative or positive reactions. Because the camera can manipulate the likeness of a person, print and other forms of media, still motivated by profit, have used lighting, pose, and attire to create whatever racist stereotype of African—African males especially—it deems appropriate. For instance, in 1990 five young black men were tried and convicted of a brutal assault on Trisha Meili in New York's Central Park. The guilty verdict was later vacated in 2002, but the media frenzy surrounding the case in 1990 created a photographic orgy. The young men had been photographed in lighting that further darkened their skin, and the solemn expressions on their faces made guilt seem all the more believable (Virginia Law Review v.52 (1966), pp. 1189–1223. Of course, they were not guilty, and another man later confessed that he had committed the crime and the DNA evidence confirmed his confession.

Furthermore, in what has been called the criminal trial of the twentieth century, a darkened photo of O. J. Simpson appeared on the cover of *Time* magazine, presenting an even more dramatic illustration of psychologically destructive African images. Although the question of why the media portrays racist stereotypes is debatable, we cannot dispute the fact that too many dark-skinned Americans are characterized, regardless of demography, by such racist images because the image creator applies the simplest form of the social narrative (Hall, 1993, pp. 239–251). Of course, in a normal racist world, only whites would find darkened photos of value. But because blacks in a racist society are also victims of the bizarre social narrative, seeing a darkened photo of O. J. Simpson demonstrates, even for blacks, that there is something negative about his character. If we had a positive view of blackness, then the photo would be celebrated for its color; alas, black is seen as negative and brutish.

Following World War II, television became more popular than radio. Its moving pictures brought images to life in a way that print or radio could not. Therefore, more than any other component of modern media, television is by far the most potent vehicle for imagery. Furthermore, since the advent of cable television, virtually every home across America has access to its airwaves. More so than print and radio, television's power is intimate and immediate.

Television's ability to drive home destructive images of Africans was politically exploited in the case of William Horton ("Bush, Gore and Willie Horton," July 15, 1992). Horton was a prisoner in Massachusetts, where he had been incarcerated for murder. Under the gubernatorial administration of then-Democratic presidential nominee Mike Dukakis, he had been granted temporary release through a weekend furlough plan, and he did not return, eventually committing assault, armed robbery, and rape. Dukasis's opponent, George H. W. Bush, seized on this incident, launching a smear campaign that featured images of Horton. There was nothing new about this old stereotype, but the "virtual reality" of television allowed viewers to pseudo-experience Horton. Bush's campaign assumed that white Americans, both male and female, would associate the negative feelings invoked by the images of Horton with Dukakis, and they would then go out and vote accordingly. In the end, Bush won the 1988 presidential campaign in part by exploiting and nurturing black stereotypes ("Bush, Gore and Willie Horton," July 15, 1992).

In a subsequent 1990 incident in Boston, Massachusetts, an African American male was accused of murdering a white housewife who was pregnant by her husband. The entire nation assumed that the accused was guilty, and based this conclusion on media hype and blown-up photographs of the murder scene. Only after one of the accomplices involved in the frame-up came forward to reveal the truth—that the white husband was the murderer—was Mr. Bennett, the alleged perpetrator, released from police custody (Theorahis and Woznica, 1990). Americans' belief that Mr. Bennett was guilty as charged was, arguably, in large part a reaction to his dark skin and race.

The 1995 case of Susan Smith of Union, South Carolina, provides a more recent and dramatic manifestation of the destructive African image perpetrated by mass media. Smith, who was later convicted of murdering her two children, initially told police and the media that she had been attacked by an African male. In the aftermath, this unknown assailant was presumed to have kidnapped her young sons when he stole her car. Well aware of the stereotype, Smith assumed that her Scottsboro-like southern town of Union, South Carolina, would not question the all-too-believable destructive image of the dark-skinned African male. Fortunately, police questioned her story. Their investigation led to the arrest and conviction of the accuser. However, the fact that an African male had, once again, been wrongly accused of a crime was lost in the popular media account of what happened. Instead, the major headlines emphasized that she drowned her two children while ignoring the indictment of an entire group of innocent citizens (Turnipseed, 2000).

Because dark skin contrasts with light skin, which is viewed as the norm, it is also necessarily vilified in the subjective assessment of guilt. African Americans remain constantly aware of that assessment in all matters of law and other public affairs. This vilification has contributed to the victimization of dark-skinned Americans (Turnipseed, 2000). Hence, in comparison to blacks with lighter skin, African Americans with darker skin are, more often than any other racial, ethnic, gender, social/culture group, falsely accused as active participants in criminal activity (Turnipseed, 2000).

For instance, a 42-year-old dentist claimed to have been pulled over by state troopers more than fifty times on the New Jersey turnpike on his commute to work. Dr. Elmo Randolph is not a careless driver. In fact, despite being frequently pulled over by police, Randolph has never been issued a ticket. Each time the state troopers pull him over, their questions are routine: "Do you have any drugs or weapons in your car?" (ACLU, 2002). Dr. Randolph drives a BMW and, being an African male, has relatively dark skin. For years, African Americans like Randolph have complained about being humiliated by racist law enforcement policies without anything being done to stop it. The police argue that race is irrelevant when being stopped on the turnpike, but in fact, skin color appears to be the basis for being stopped according to three African Americans and one Latino American, all of whom were shot by state troopers.

As the four males drove along the turnpike in a rented van, police pulled them over and opened fire, striking three of the males and critically wounding two of them. At police headquarters, officers contended the suspects were stopped because radar showed the van to be traveling at an excessive rate of speed. The department where the officers were stationed was forced to admit later that they had no radar equipment. The circumstances for the shooting were assessed via investigation.

The most troubling aspect of this New Jersey incident, aside from the shootings, is the fact that no less than three years earlier, a New Jersey judge concluded that troopers were practicing racial profiling. Instead of doing what was necessary to eradicate such racism from the ranks of law enforcement, the Attorney General, in a political maneuver, sided with the troopers to appeal the case. After the public became aware of the case, however, the Attorney General declined to pursue the case because he was concerned about winning a political office.

This New Jersey case indicates that racism reaches every level of the American judicial system, extending to African Americans regardless of status, and is a constant source of stress otherwise unknown to law-abiding white citizens. That the problem in New Jersey is so pervasive is exemplified by the fact that the U.S. Justice Department decided it would intervene if the New Jersey governor decided to ignore it.

Destructive images of African folk prevail into the present. In April of 2006, according to Kevin Grasha of Michigan's *Lansing State Journal* newspaper (2006), an African male was accused of shooting a local police officer. The alleged victim was a sergeant on the force who, in fact, was not shot by an African male but, in actuality, according to prosecutors, shot himself. The alleged victim's name is Sgt. Jeff Lutz of the Eaton County, Michigan Sheriff's department. According to Lutz, a little after 3 a.m., he was shot in his right arm while patrolling in the vicinity of West Town Plaza located near West Saginaw Highway. Immediately, the local police took control of neighborhoods and school buildings as they conducted a massive manhunt that extended into daybreak. An estimated 40 or more police officers on loan from approximately six area departments along with a helicopter participated in the manhunt.

The department where the victim worked released a description of the assailant to the news media. He described him as an African male, about six feet tall, with "muscles." He looked to be in his mid-20s and, relative to white Americans, has a dark skin color with "pock marks" about his face. Unfortunately, this description was also inaccurate because the shooting, as told by the officer, was a deliberate fabrication. The police department had released an artist's sketch of the fabricated assailant that it has since retracted. To ensure an objective investigation, the local department turned the case over to the Michigan State Police. Eaton County's police department insisted that it had acted with the "highest professional standards."

Sgt. Lutz was charged with filing a false report that led to a massive manhunt for the fictitious African suspect. The officer was arraigned in the Eaton County District Court. He faced a maximum sentence of four years in the penitentiary for the two felonies with which he was charged. He was also liable for any costs incurred by other agencies that responded to calls to help apprehend the culprit. After the farce, Lutz was placed under observation at a local hospital.

The destructive images of the African male today have led many Americans to believe that black males are criminals, fathers of illegitimate children, unmotivated, ill-educated, unintelligible, jobless, unemployable, and dangerous. We argue that beginning in infancy, blacks are saturated with destructive images projected not only from whites but other blacks as well. African children then internalize these images that have the potential to lead them to feel self-hate, which may result in political conservatism. This conclusion is based soundly in empirical evidence.

Research has confirmed that destructive African images are prevalent among some African Americans. According to a 1990 survey involving racial attitudes conducted by the National Opinion Research Center, 30 percent of the blacks taking part agreed to the suggestion that blacks were less intelligent than whites. In comparison, a total of 57 percent of whites agreed to this suggestion (Rowan, Pernell, and Akers, 1995, p. 1).

The psychological problems blacks face border on what some have described as perceptual genocide. Black social scientists have identified the media as one of the major institutions that help perpetuate this perceptual distortion. As McAdoo (1987) pointed out, the media rarely portrays blacks as ordinary citizens but rather tends to portray them in attention-grabbing circumstances or situations, such as athletes or criminals. McAdoo additionally showed how readily films feature African males in criminal and illegal drug activities. McAdoo's assertions are confirmed by a recently cited study by the National Rainbow Coalition Commission on "Fairness in Media," which found that African Americans appear on the news as criminals twice as often as do other racial groups (Cole, 1995, p. 10A). In response to such racial bias in media, black men and women succumb to a host of psychological disorders.

The Token Black Syndrome (TBS) disorder was devised by psychologist Price Cobbs to address the psychological disposition of the black conservative. Commensurate with self-hate, TBS is a disease that afflicts African conservatives who may have been the first member of their families to get a college education or find employment doing prestigious work. TBS, according to Cobbs has become more prevalent in the post–Civil Rights era in response to white objections to Affirmative Action. Affected blacks fear that, in the eyes of white Americans, their hire is not needed and that they will fail to meet the same standards of performance as a white worker.

In the aftermath of constant assaults on the African psyche, psychiatrist Alvin Poussaint contends that African conservatives have unconsciously internalized the destructive images of African people they are exposed to on a daily basis. In response, they separate themselves in every way possible from what America despises, and this is apparent in their words, deeds, and politics. African conservatives so affected will deny that luck, family, or Affirmative Action had anything to do with their success in life. Instead, they are convinced that their appointment to the Supreme Court or as Secretary of State is purely a matter of individual talents and hard work. They are convinced of their superiority and that the masses of less fortunate blacks are underclass because they are inferior. Such black conservatives express acute disdain for those blacks who they criticize for being on welfare or having children out of wedlock. They believe that if more blacks were conservatives, they too would reflect the qualities of a black conservative Supreme Court Justice, that is, intelligent, hard working, educated, and morally upright (White, Ludtke, and Winbush, September 16, 1991).

The racial progress made in America has not directly benefited blacks psychologically even when they have attained a quality of education that would lead them to a Supreme Court bench. In their article, "Race the Pain of Being Black," White, Ludtke, and Winbush quoted Gloria Johnson-Powell, an African psychiatrist at Harvard. She referred to a case study from the early 1980s conducted by psychiatrists, psychologists, and social workers that demonstrated that in a number of areas, African professionals in America internalized more stereotypical negative images of African folk than their corresponding white peers. Johnson-Powell said, "Some African American professionals look down their nose at another African American who is a shame to the race. They swallow the stereotypes and often will be harder on African Americans than whites will be" (White, Ludtke, and Winbush, *Time*, 1991, September 16, p. 12).

In the event that an African conservative is able to bypass the assaults on the African psyche and emerge without dysfunction, what he or she may recall makes it abundantly clear that the psychological pressures that have destroyed other blacks are not a product of blacks' imagination. The most well-adjusted and self-confident blacks cannot escape the fear that their performance in the company of whites is being assessed using a different measuring device than that applied to other whites. Especially painful is that such blacks suspect that they are taking part in some grand experiment in which their performance will be used to assess the entire African race, a suspicion that serves as a strong motivating factor for action. For those blacks who succeed in spite of the circumstances of being African in America, they are then judged as an exception; if they fail, the prevailing rationale is that this is what whites expected.

As descendants of field Negroes, most African Americans have been inclined to identify themselves politically as progressive or, in some instances, what today might be termed *liberal*. Although liberal did not always directly address the issues that were most significant to Africans in general, unlike conservative politics, African issues could be addressed within a liberal political context. In the aftermath of a sizable mixed-race, light-skinned population, the political lines within the African community gradually separated less on the basis of skin color and more on the basis of psychological disposition, which for African conservatives could be determined by white conservative influence. African Americans might often have identified themselves as conservative, whether light skinned or dark skinned, and preferred the life and values of the antebellum house Negroes who invested their entire efforts politically in satisfying the master's wishes.

The condition of many blacks is the stain of poor cultural esteem created by the overarching canopy of racist images. Theories have been put forward not only by white but also African scholars to explain the black condition.

They include among the most noted: social identity theory, social exchange theory, and the social equity hypothesis, which supports the contention of African self-hate as a form of a more general cultural problem (Crocker and Major, 1989, pp. 608–630). Although numerous articles substantiate the existence of low cultural esteem, we should not assume that all blacks suffer cultural negativity or self-dysfunction. However, those blacks whose political preferences approximate that of the white conservative do offer evidence of deep trauma around African culture. In most cases, they neither speak nor write of an appreciation for African culture, either on the continent or in the Diaspora, because they see it as representing the most negative existential aspects of their existence.

Morris Rosenberg, a leading theorist of the self, provided two major reasons to explain why African Americans might succumb to self-hate: First, prejudice against African Americans in the United States has endured since the antebellum, thus making it virtually impossible to understand how such persons could not self-hate; and second, statistical facts, including rates of unemployment, education, and other quality-of-life measures, ensure self-doubt and self-hate. The research on African self-hate is so extensive that many scholars accept it as a fact of black history (Crocker and Major, 1989, p. 630). They reference a report conducted by Cartwright (Crocker and Major, 1989, pp. 610–611) that validates the contention that self-hatred is likely to be associated with membership in lowly regarded groups, of which African Americans belong by virtue of the oppression created by enslavement and segregation (pp. 608–630). Furthermore, the pioneering race theorist Gordon Allport (1958, p. 213) contended that "group oppression may destroy the integrity of the ego entirely, and reverse its normal pride, and create a groveling self-image."

Kenneth Clark and Mamie Clark conducted perhaps the most stunning research when they investigated the significance of psychological problems of black children in the well-known series of "doll studies" (Clark and Clark, 1980, pp. 159–169). In an effort to confront school segregation, Clark and Clark directed most of their studies at segregated southern schools. A few northern schools were consulted to validate southern findings, which resulted in the same conclusions concerning black self-hate. Astoundingly, the African American researchers discovered that racial recognition in both black and white children is evident as soon as the third year and becomes increasingly sophisticated as they get older. Among the most dramatic evidence found in all of these studies is African children's tendency to idealize white skin when queried. Their racial sophistication lags behind that of white children, but they do coincide. For example, despite being black, African children more often preferred white dolls and white friends. They may identify themselves as white or reveal a reluctance to embrace their blackness. Taken in unison, African and white children both associate blacks with poverty, poorer houses, and anything less desirable (Clark and Clark, 1980, pp. 159–165).

As black children age, their tendency to self-hate begins to wane, although there does remain evidence of some residual affects. Another study of children aged 8 to 13 years of age enrolled at a summer camp observed that African camp goers were initially oversensitive to unfavorable behavior of their black peers (White, Ludtke, and Winbush, 1991, September 16). They tended to avoid making other black friends. However, once the children were exposed to an egalitarian, interracial setting, such inclinations tended to terminate. Thus, in as little as two weeks, an interracial camping experience can significantly alter African self-hate in African children (White, Ludtke, and Winbush, September 16, 1991). Of course, the Afrocentric school movement has demonstrated that the children who are placed in a positive African American environment in school and taught the history of African people will make a dramatic improvement in self- and cultural image.

By the time blacks reach adolescence, dating becomes an intense issue—not only for blacks but whites as well. However, for African children raised in the North, where segregation has been less overt, dating represents a turning point in their white friendships. The onset of puberty means that the African child will no longer be invited to his white friends' birthday or other parties. At that point, the white parents' racist fears surface, and the African adolescent is forced to resolve the situation in a way that does not damage his or her self-esteem. For those raised in the segregated South, where they may not even have white friends, they still experience an identity crisis nevertheless. White school teachers, peer group information, contact with the white world combine to emotionally shock African adolescents. The omnipotent denigration of all manners of blackness combines to severely and emotionally cripple the African psyche. The self-hatred often evident in the African conservative is the end result of a phalanx of negativity about blackness.

Because of circumstances, many African adolescents manage to endure early life still able to succeed as young adults. If they do, there are many challenges they must still face, such as employment discrimination and housing segregation. When whites deny them a job in favor of a less-qualified white applicant, or a seller refuses an offer to purchase a house well within their budget, they once again face the task of assessing their self-worth and their status within the world. The childhood issues long suppressed may resurface, which results in newfound sources of stress that were once thought resolved.

Scientists know that the destructive images faced by African Americans are commensurate with problems of self-esteem leading to self-hate. Historically, Africans have had little else by which to assess themselves other than the distorted views of mainstream white America. For instance, in popular texts such as *The Bell Curve* by Richard Herrnstein and Charles Murray, African inferiority is assumed as fact (Jacoby and Glauberman, 1995). These assaults on black people by racist social scientists often become indistinguishable from the works of other white scholars. In the aftermath, blacks may consciously or subconsciously internalize accusations of their inferiority. In a capitalistic society, they too value "status" and "success." But when they attempt to apply these values to themselves, they find failure, which results in self-hate. In whatever competition with whites, except for some athletic exceptions, blacks may feel incompetent or lack the necessary confidence to succeed. Research suggests that even when blacks are equal to whites in intellect and skill level, some may nevertheless feel inferior to their white counterpart.

For white Americans not similarly abused by destructive images of themselves, it is difficult for them to grasp the significance of African self-hate. It is a matter that cannot be accurately conveyed by text or verbiage. Although African self-hatred today is not as extensive as it was in the 1950s or the antebellum, its implications are apparent in a much-changed America. According to writer James Baldwin,

> the American Negro can no longer, nor will he ever again, be controlled by white America's image of him. This fact has everything to do with the rise of Africa in world affairs. At the time that I was growing up, Negroes in this country were taught to be ashamed of Africa.... One was always being mercilessly scrubbed and polished, as though in the hope that a stain could

thus be washed away. . . . The women were forever straightening and curling their hair, and using bleaching creams. . . . But none of this is so for those who are young now ... by the time they were able to react to the world, Africa was on the stage of history. This could not but have an extraordinary effect on their own morale, for it meant that they were not merely the descendants of enslaved Africans in a white Protestant, and Puritan country: they were also related to kings and princes in an ancestral homeland far away. And this has proved to be a great antidote to the poison of self-hatred. (Pettigrew, 1964, pp. 13–35)

Black conservatives do not embrace Baldwin's notion of "kings and princes" in Africa and, thus, continue on in their futile struggles with pathological manifestations of self-hatred that can never release them from the bondage of white racial domination. They might even claim that "kings and queens" of the past cannot do anything for you now in the twenty-first century, but the masses of black folk know that the best medicine for negativity is to demonstrate that their conditions were not always this way. Embracing one's ancestors is the only method for reinforcing collectivity and shared histories; the black conservative is eager to take that away from the black masses because they recognize the power, not the impotence, of that idea.

According to clinical social worker Ronald E. Hall, submission to the all-powerful white father is so extensive among black conservatives that victims undergo the "bleaching syndrome," in which they "de-stain" themselves of anything African and deny any association with the masses of African people at all. They might be willing to take on all of their "other" histories or ethnicities, but the black one remains a real stain that they want to remove. Of course, if they had a positive view of Africa, they would embrace it gladly and without any hint of shame or guilt.

The concept of the Bleaching Syndrome in regard to African conservatives grew out of the idea that every individual has aspirations and wants to improve their station in life. It is a theoretical tool that describes in a logical order the complex process of self-hate and its impact on the politics/socialization of victim groups. Much of what can be described is behavioral, but a considerable amount takes the form of psychological phenomena, which is manifested by way of the African conservative's self-hate. The syndrome is associated with a number of critical social systems—such as the family—and societal institutions—such as politics. The Bleaching

Syndrome orders these factors in a way that is as close to the objectivity of mathematics as possible. Furthermore, the Bleaching Syndrome conforms to and enhances the well-established "person in the environment" approach to human behavior because it is able to explain more social phenomena.

The genesis of the Bleaching Syndrome is historically rooted in old beauty creams and preparations that African folk used to make their skin lighter. The word "bleach" is a verb that means "to remove color or to make white." A "syndrome" consists of a grouping of symptoms, that is, behaviors that occur in conjunction with each other and comprise a recognizable pattern. In combination, historical evidence and English terminology literally define the Bleaching Syndrome. Because of its universality, it is also a metaphor. Its relevancy to the African conservative in the aftermath of the antebellum period is universal because its application is limitless. But, when applied to African conservatives, its existence is substantiated in a most dramatic fashion. These black conservatives have had to idealize norms, which are often radically inconsistent with their uninterrogated cultural traditions and outward appearances; often, once they come to terms with their historical identity, they feel angry and disappointed because society has denied them their right to know their own ancestors. Furthermore, the psychological pain they suffer is exacerbated by America's general lack of acceptance or tolerance for its growing diversity.

African conservatives' efforts to please the white father power structure and simultaneously reduce psychological pain are made possible by their obsession with a "bleached" ideal. The presence of that ideal is manifested in their internalization of all things white and their separation from and denigration of all things black. No other aspect of African self-hate is more personally revealing.

Psychologically, the Bleaching Syndrome involves the conscious and systematic process of self-hatred and aspiration to idealized white conservative norms at the expense of psychological health. Their ultimate objective is to attain a desired quality of life that can only be realized by acceptance into the white conservative mainstream. Given the disparities of power, African Americans are not in a position to negotiate. This is psychologically painful and becomes a strong incentive for internalizing conservative ideals in spite of impending pathologies. The process involves a linear progression of stages consisting of power, domination, assimilation, and, ultimately, the Bleaching Syndrome. It has three components, which consist of the following: (A) perceptual, according to internalized ideals; (B) psychological, according to reactions to those ideals; and (C) behavioral, according to the ideals manifested.

The Bleaching Syndrome among African conservatives is also a conscious awareness of the cognitive and attitudinal levels of the similarities and differences between the dominant political mainstream and the dominated African community as well as the need to negate themselves in order to be accepted into the fold of conservative white society. The quality of life this may infer, according to Abraham Maslow, the motivational theorist, fulfills such physiological needs as wealth and income as well as such safety needs as housing and standard of living. Belongingness, self-esteem, and self-actualization needs are secondary to the African conservative, which means that the Bleaching Syndrome prevents them from advancing beyond the base of Maslow's hierarchy. It requires substantive knowledge and empathic appreciation of white culture at the expense of African self-esteem. Thus, the Bleaching Syndrome suggests that African conservatives affected by it must alter themselves to approximate a conservative political white fantasy. Such alteration is a quasi-functional strategy, one that ultimately fails.

The Bleaching Syndrome is a self-hating process of orientation that requires a disparity in power. Were it not for the differential in power between African folk and their white American counterparts, it could not exist. Much of what the Bleaching Syndrome requires is pathological to the African community and could not otherwise be imposed because it is contrary to their physical, emotional, and psychological health. Black conservatives may manifest the Bleaching Syndrome in their values, interactional styles, behavioral responses, language use, and, most importantly, politics. It is a distortion of Maslow's hierarchy of needs (Zastrow and Kirst-Ashman, 1990). Such impositions are not only psychologically destructive but also painful in the way they inflict damage. The intensity of their pain may subside over time, but the ultimate ill effects are not lessened.

Supreme Court Justice Clarence Thomas is a prime example of a black person who essentially supports the agenda of the conservative movement while undermining the historical movement of black people, women, and other "special" groups' efforts to gain liberation and progressive rights. Being *Clarencised*, that is, being distanced from one's own family, community, or national history, is a process that happens over years, as the black person relinquishes more and more of his own historical and cultural ground.

The pain that racist society causes when persecuting the psyche persists even when a person holds a high office. Thus, to be *Clarencised* is to exist with this burden of racial damage inflicted by segregation, apartheid, or other forms of identity crushing. The term became common after Clarence Thomas was appointed to the Supreme Court.

Justice Thomas is by birth a Southerner raised at a time when dignity and self-respect were an illusion to African folk. Initially, Thomas aspired to become a member of the clergy in an effort to please his rigid, authoritarian grandfather. Like many African Americans, his life story of struggle is not unique; in fact, under the circumstances, it is quite common. Most African Americans fortunate enough to experience some measure of success in life can attribute that success to family members who had less. For many, there is someone like Clarence Thomas's grandfather, who, though he could not succeed himself, found his success in the next generation. Yet conservatives are often rigid and unyielding, convinced that blacks who fail do so by their own means, are lazy, or without values. Thus, if they want, blacks can succeed, as they have, by their own means, which is usually only half true. No person succeeds without others, but the conservatives seek to minimize racial discrimination by considering it a part of normal society. The role of racism and African oppression in quality of life becomes irrelevant to the conservatives.

A brief investigation of Justice Thomas's life will reveal the self-hate that has manifested his tendencies that led him to become a black conservative. That self-hate is a product of a history of destructive images portraying him personally, his family, his community, and his worth as a human being as negative. It is a psychological consequence of the progress some have made, especially in recent generations. Some may applaud Thomas's success, and white conservatives in particular insist that Thomas is a prime example of what all worthy African folk should aspire to in order to improve their lot. Unfortunately, however, there are other aspects of Justice Thomas that pertain to his psychological development in a racist society that supporters are less likely to comment on publicly. Such aspects reveal an African man who appears to have been damaged by the destructive images of Africans that have been internalized since childhood. Enabled by the influence of an authoritarian dictatorial grandfather, Thomas is a classic example of African self-hate in not only the way he regards African people but also members of his own family. Even African conservatives have acknowledged the shortcomings of Thomas's life. Shelby Steele has described Thomas's problematic psyche as "integration shock." According to Steele, evidence of integration shock is manifested as "intense feelings of racial inferiority and self-doubt" on the part of successful African Americans (quoted in Hall, 2010, p. 50). Similar to culture shock, blacks are thrust into an all-white world, where they do not have the cultural skills to survive and are also subjected to overt hostilities. Evidence of the resulting self-hate has been investigated extensively in scholarly literature.

Steele, who has experienced his own shock of African culture, is not alone in his assessment of Justice Thomas's self-hate psyche. Psychiatrists have long known of the prevailing impact that a racist society has on the house Negro African conservative. Each victim may respond differently. Symptomology may range from an angry denial of white oppression, as is the case with African conservatives, to an emotional attachment to whites as the rigid father with whom they identify, which is also indicative of the African conservative.

Justice Clarence Thomas grew up in the 1950s. Due to his dark, field Negro–like skin color, he was ridiculed by friends as "A.B.C.," an acronym for America's Blackest Child. Both African and white children in his Southern Georgia town referred to him by this name. In the 1950s, prior to the "Black is beautiful" Movement, "A.B.C." was the cruelest of nicknames an African child could have. What's more, as the only African student enrolled in a southern Catholic boarding school, Thomas was the butt of unimaginable racist insults on a daily basis. When the lights are out at night, white students might yell for all to hear: "Smile, Clarence, so we can see you" (White, Ludtke, and Winbush, 1991, September 16, pp. 1–3). Thomas himself has admitted to a period when he felt self-hate, which, as a black conservative, he projected onto other blacks. When submitting to whites failed, he assumed there was little he could do to earn their respect. However, because of his skin color, Thomas found little sympathy in the African community and experienced other manifestations of ridicule on a daily basis.

The destructive images associated with skin color are not irrelevant to African conservatives such as Thomas, and this is made evident through an examination of African terminology. For instance, the folk terms used to designate skin color variations include for light skin such complimentary references as "high-yellow," "ginger," "creme-colored" and "bronze"

(Herskovits, 1963). Blacks use similar references to designate features associated with light skin. They include hair, which is designated as "bad" if it is the kinky, African-type characteristic of those who have dark skin, and it is "good" if it is the straight, Caucasian-type characteristic of those who have light skin. And before the "Black is Beautiful" movement, the term *black* more often than not designated something threatening and sinister, particularly if it involved an African male (R. L. Jones, 1980). Justice Thomas is a dark-skinned African male with kinky African hair, features that did not serve his attempts to escape his tendency to self-hate.

Shortly after the Garvey era, overt verbal hostilities regarding skin color largely subsided in the African community. Associating light skin with the societal ideal, however, continued and actually became more accepted over time, as can be seen in some of the rituals of African youth that victimized Thomas (Kroeger, 2003). On the college campus, it was almost impossible for a dark-skinned student to join a black sorority or fraternity. Various social events such as school dances required the "brown-paper-bag test" as a condition of admission. Those individuals darker than a brown paper bag would have to pay, whereas those lighter-skinned were admitted free of charge (Hall, 2003). Such ridicule may, in fact, have resulted in Thomas's decision to attend a white university rather than an HBCU (historically African college) closer to home. In doing so, he might escape the taunts of his African friends for his dark skin color.

The rhetoric of the 1960s espoused healthier norms in the African community (Hall, 2003). Kinky hair and dark features were heralded as desirable on the campus and in marriage. In retrospect, however, what was practiced did not always coincide with what was preached. Dark-skinned students could join fraternities and sororities, but such persons did not appear to be able to overcome the denigration of dark skin (Hall, 2003). Still, the issue of skin color was seldom discussed openly or at a public form.

Although Justice Thomas did not initially admit to self-hate during his life growing up, his attempts to separate himself from African people are obvious in his social life, education, and, most importantly, conservative political views. While enrolled at Yale law school, Thomas made every effort to avoid law classes on civil rights issues. Instead, he chose classes more likely to interest whites, such as classes on corporate law. Following graduation, Thomas resented offers from firms that worked for African or other good causes. He eventually accepted a position in the Missouri state attorney general's office. There, where he handled revenue and tax litigation, he saw few blacks. Soon after, the Reagan administration called, wanting to assign Thomas to the Department of Education as Assistant Secretary for Civil Rights. In that position, his self-hate in being compared to African folk became a matter of public record. He insisted that Africans who accepted welfare were engaging in little more than a "sugar-coated form of slavery" (White, Ludtke, and Winbush, 1991, September 16, pp. 1–2).

Thomas's African conservative friends think of him as a well-adjusted African man who displays self-esteem and a keen intellect, but of course, many of these blacks suffer from the same syndrome. One can understand why they do not see his conservative politics as an opportunity to profit at the expense of Africans, nor do they see him as an "Uncle Tom," as others contend. They would not see themselves as Uncle Toms or Aunt Jemimas either, terms that a majority of black people may use to describe them. However, contrary to their views, Thomas has exemplified his self-hate and hatred of African people in his negative evaluation of his own family members.

In 1980 Justice Thomas attended a meeting of African conservatives in San Francisco, California. During that meeting, Thomas publicly referred to his sister Emma Martin as an example of what happens when blacks depend on liberal programs such as welfare: "'She gets mad when the mailman is late with her welfare check, that's how dependent she is,' said Thomas. 'What's worse is that now her kids feel entitled to the check too. They have no motivation for doing better or getting out of that situation'" (White, Ludtke, and Winbush, 1991, September 16, p. 2). In fact, as is frequently the African conservative modus operandi, Thomas's version of his sister's situation narrates the details creatively. At the time of the San Francisco meeting, his sister was not on welfare but rather working double shifts at a nursing home for little more than a mere $2 per hour. At various times in her life, she had relied on welfare, such as when she left an abusive marriage or when she had to care for an ailing family member. Furthermore, even when she was on welfare, Thomas's sister maintained part-time employment, picking crabmeat at a factory near her residence. At some point when she was getting off welfare, Thomas's sister obtained two low-paying jobs to support herself. After learning how her brother had publicly denigrated her, Thomas's sister refused to respond critically.

African people who are less affected by self-hate may, at some point, have felt critical of a family member, but they would never have made their feelings public, particularly for a white audience. But African conservatives do not embrace their blackness. Most likely, in Thomas's psyche, he is among the mainstream white population, given his obvious disdain for Africans. Even more white in his family norms, blacks not consumed by self-hate as Thomas would have attempted to help a family member like a sister who, due to circumstances beyond her control, required welfare as a temporary source of financial support.

Although the politics of skin color remain acutely relevant to politics of the African conservative, the public has generally not acknowledged the issues surrounding skin color because of Eurocentric influences. Conversely, African folk are astutely aware of its existence, as those among African conservatives act out its pathologies politically through the issues they advocate, the legislation they address, and the political candidates they support. Thus, by African conservative standards, in an effort to escape social ridicule and self-hate, fighting the oppression of Africans is not an urgent issue. In fact, African conservatives assume that people who fail in life or are systematically abused in various ways must address their personal shortcomings and not expect the government to compensate for their lack of personal responsibility. However, there exists a direct correlation between the destructive images of Africans, no less traditional than they were in the antebellum, and self-hate. African conservatism is one manifestation of this self-hate, whereas others succumb to drugs, welfare, or dysfunctional families. However, in all instances, self-hate is evident as a vehicle perpetuating social ills otherwise unnecessary.

African conservatives' ability to perceive, conceptualize, and interact willingly with the underclass of the African people will be a formidable challenge to the viability of African people as a whole. They must acknowledge past oppression in the African community so as to validate the pain encountered by a less fortunate majority who many African conservatives despise. Black conservatives must gain the strength to confront and, when necessary, challenge the political objectives of a conservative white power structure that they regard as a rigid, authoritarian father figure. Otherwise, their lack of self-pride and self-esteem will pale in the face of destructive, superior political forces. Black conservatives will continue to operate as tools to oppress their own people, who, for lack of their support, remain victim to conservative political agendas. Furthermore, at a time of increased contacts between various populations, the African conservative is confronted by issues and perspectives that did not require intellectual consideration in the past (Shatz, September 2, 2001, p. 11). African conservatives are, therefore, also challenged to develop creative strategies that are not as confined by white racial bias. Without racial bias, the tyranny of conservative politics will then dissolve the self-hate that is evident among African conservatives and that is necessary for the democratic process to evolve civilly.

# CHAPTER SIX

## *Extending the Metaphors*

### Conservatives and Liberals

Life for African Americans has always existed in concert with the risks brought about by constant discrimination and institutionalized oppression. In various ways, different factions of the African community at various times have attempted to challenge this oppression so as to acquire the same rights and privileges as white people. Some blacks who have attained wealth, such as professional athletes or entertainers, have managed to buy at least a few of the trappings of dignity, such as purchasing a house in a more upscale neighborhood or sending their children to private schools. Although such blacks are noted for being very visible, they are by far the prevailing exception to the rule. Indeed, although many professional blacks appear to have finally acquired the American Dream that was unavailable to their ancestors who arrived via the European Slave Trade, at any minute they could once again face the perils of field Negroes, whether by harassment at their jobs, discrimination in their salaries, or rude awakenings about social relationships. An example of this occurs when white physicians discriminate against African American cardiologists when referring patients. You might have the ability and the credentials to be a top surgeon, but if white physicians do not refer their patients to you, your practice suffers because there are far more white doctors than black.

Thus, disappointment with racist treatment often drives African Americans to consider abandoning their own culture and style or their professions. They become victims in much the same way as enslaved Africans became victims during the years of plantation living. Or they wrestle so blindly with self-hatred that they descend into an oblivion almost unreachable by normal reasoning. Consider the plight of Anne Wortham, perhaps one of the most representative black female darlings of the Right. We use quotation marks for the term because Wortham had once claimed to prefer the term *Negro,* as in house Negro, or *colored* to the terms *black* or *African American.* However, since the election of President Barack Obama, she has been using the term *black* in order to identify her credentials to criticize his election as having nothing to do with her. For example, she wrote on November 6, 2008, under the title "No He Can't," the following statement to her "Fellow Americans":

> Please know: I am black; I grew up in the segregated South. I did not vote for Barack Obama; I wrote in Ron Paul's name as my choice for president. Most importantly, I am not race conscious. I do not require a black president to know that I am a person of worth, and that life is worth living. I do not require a black president to love the ideal of America. I cannot join you in your celebration. I feel no elation. There is no smile on my face. I am not jumping with joy. There are no tears of triumph in my eyes. For such emotions and behavior to come from me, I would have to deny all that I know about the requirements of human flourishing and survival—all that I know about the history of the United States of America, all that I know about American race relations, and all that I know about Barack Obama as a politician. I would have to deny the nature of the "change" that Obama asserts has come to America. Most importantly, I would have to abnegate my certain understanding that you have chosen to sprint down the road to serfdom that we have been on for over a century. I would have to pretend that individual liberty has no value for the success of a human life. (Wortham, 2008, November 6)

Wortham can find "no elation" from the election of Barack Obama and she is not "race conscious." Whatever damage inflicted by the vicissitudes of living in America, one thing is quite clear: She is either a great prevaricator or she has lost all attachment to reality—and both are decidedly crippling when it comes to open communication. Even white American conservatives, despite themselves, have remarked that although they differed with Obama politically, they felt joy knowing how the nation's consciousness had grown as we elected an African American. For a black person to say that they are not "race conscious" means that they are only "white" conscious as the default position in American society is white and European. In a racist society, one can never divest oneself of some kind of race consciousness. This does not mean that you have to be a racist, but to be antiracist means that you have to have some form of race consciousness.

Perhaps even more striking is when Wortham stated that if she felt any emotion, any elation about the election of Barack Obama, "I would have to abnegate my certain understanding that you have chosen to sprint down the road to serfdom that we have been on for over a century." Here, she refers to the entire twentieth century, commencing about 45 years after the enslavement of African people ended. How could "we" have been "sprinting down the road to serfdom" when black people, if anything, fought in every conceivable way to expand the boundaries of freedom that had come only partially in 1865 with the end of the Civil War. Alas, Wortham is identifying herself with the white "we" just as the house Negroes did during the antebellum period. Because she is "not race conscious," she does not understand that during the nadir, when the practice of lynching black people took on monstrous proportions, we had heroic individuals like Ida B. Wells Barnett, Anna Julia Cooper, the Grimkes, and others who took up the fight against the most devious enemies a people had ever faced in a democracy. Because Wortham declared that she is "not race conscious," she cannot appreciate the horrendous difficulties that A. Philip Randolph and James Weldon Johnson had to confront when organizing the black masses, the descendants of the field Negroes. But because Wortham has little regard for this history and for the work of her ancestors as they fought enslavement, discrimination, prejudice, lynching, and injustice, she cannot glory in the election of Barack Obama, regardless of politics. Seeing and reading her position on the election is one of the most awesome revelations about the spiritual inheritance of the black conservative.

## Black Conservatives: A Minority Within

Some blacks became politically conservative as a "new" strategy in their quest to live the American Dream. In the aftermath of the 1960s Civil Rights Movement, a white backlash brought into existence a highly concerted conservative and energetic reaction to what were considered black advances in the social and political realm. This ideological reaction, led by intellectuals such as William Buckley and George Wills, with some aspects of Ayn Rand's philosophy thrown in to grease the arguments, dominated the southern white political spectrum during the late 1970s and early 1980s. Ronald Reagan, an actor who rose to become the governor of California and then the president of the United States, solidified for many whites and a vocal minority of black conservatives the new dispensation. This movement distanced itself from Civil Rights by seeking to modify the language of justice by adopting the strategy of reversing the successful language of the justice movement. Indeed, racism became reverse racism, and affirmative action became affirmative reaction, and Black Power became white power, and so forth. Lynching African men at the public squares, murdering Civil Rights workers, denying black men and women the right to vote, closing down black businesses by law or by fire, bombing Tulsa's black community, killing the four little girls in the Birmingham church, and accepting the wicked discrimination of blacks by the police and other established institutions were all practices rarely mentioned, as the conservatives made the case that individual rights, not group rights, had to be ensured.

By cleverly turning the justice movement on its head, we were brought to the point at which blacks who may have been seeking justification for their lukewarm support of Civil Rights, most likely because they were scared they would be economically injured, claimed to be more for individual rights than group rights. They became black conservatives. Although we had rarely had black freedom fighters seeking only their own individual rights, this new development in our ethnic and national history heralded a neo-house Negro syndrome that would challenge and modify the more historic Civil Rights organizations. These black conservatives would come to question Barack Obama's legitimacy at all levels and rush to condemn anyone who articulated a powerful message of courage and innovation. They felt disdain because of their interpretation of African American history. For example, the black conservatives have adopted some of the same racist arguments about blacks as their white conservative allies. They share a similar ideology about the cause of discrimination, prejudice, poverty, and oppression. They have become the antivoice to Obama, whom they see as an extension of the Civil Rights Movement. Although this is not true, what is true is that Obama has never rejected and could not reasonably reject, as the black conservatives seem capable of doing, the heroic deeds of the Civil Rights Movement.

With the exception of Anne Wortham, the leading black conservatives have been black men, such as Ward Connelly, Walter Williams, Shelby Steele, Glenn Loury, Thomas Sowell, Stephen Carter, John McWhorter, and Robert Woodson. Sowell is the elder statesman of the movement, having been a confidant of many white conservatives and the first black superstar intellectual in conservative economics.

One of the most telling facts about the black conservative movement, however, is that it exists in the same ratio as the house Negroes existed to the field Negroes on a plantation the size of George Washington's: about 2 to every 100. Although we have not made a survey of overall numbers, we know that the visible black conservatives represent just a handful of individuals. For example, in addition to Thomas Sowell, an economist at the Hoover Institute, there is also Glenn Loury, an economist at Boston University; Stephen Carter at Yale University; Shelby Steele at San Jose State University; Melvin L. Williams, administrator; Gary Franks, politician; Walter Williams, economist at George Mason University; Robert Woodson, National Center for Neighborhood Enterprise; Alan Keyes, politician; Joseph Perkins, journalist; Deroy Murdock, journalist; Eileen Gardener, Heritage Foundation; Kevin Pritchett, former editor-in-chief of the *Dartmouth Review*; Claudia Butts, Heritage Foundation; William B. Allen, U.S. Civil Rights Commission; Samuel Pierce, Housing and Urban Development; and Michael Steele, head of the Republican National Committee.

The black conservatives have rarely had any ideas except to assault the Civil Rights establishment, which in fact does not exist as an establishment but is rather a group of individuals and institutions whose legacy as activists, often collectively but also singularly, is long and noble. The black conservatives' main point of contention seems to be that the continued oppression of African people, which they would call something quite different, is today little more than a historical myth because it no longer exists as a dynamic of the African political reality. Much to the contrary, however, although the face of African oppression has been modified, the dysfunctional quality of African life has not been reduced significantly; instead, it has been transformed. The vehicle for their new, more modern version of discrimination in the African community is characterized by appealing to the iconic election of Barack Obama as president as proof that racism is over.

But many people, especially unapologetic racists and the victims of racism, know that this is not true. Black conservatives now use Obama's election to advance their own agenda, because otherwise the election would end their agenda. They must demonstrate that they are just as critical of Obama as they have been of Civil Rights leaders, that is, Jesse Jackson, Al Sharpton, and the head of the venerable NAACP and the Urban League.

Although, with the election of Barack Obama to the presidency in 2008, it is true that American politics have become increasingly complex, in other ways the politics that brought him into office also continued to dominate the political structure—the ideological superstructure of the white power community. This is not simply about the numbers but rather about the political objectives of the nation. How will Obama be able to introduce and conduct a progressive political policy given a heavily conservative-influenced political legislative body? In addition, what would the ascendancy of Michael Steele, the first black, to the head of the Republican Party mean for this new American politics? Will the discrimination against blacks in the public and private sectors decrease because of these developments? We have already seen that black conservatives have responded with incredulity at the election of Obama. They believed that the Democratic Party would never elect a black candidate because the black community, the descendant of the field Negro collective from the time of enslavement, assured their support for the party, which did not, in return, have to perform for black interests. Thus, the conservatives pursued a world in which the individual black could rise, but only apart from the group, as an exceptional person.

We are sure of one thing about conservative beliefs: The circumstances for African oppression have more to do with the choices made by individual Africans rather than some systemic form of discrimination. Having relocated to the urban North for work in the smoke stack industries during the industrialization period, African Americans encountered a host of systemic social and economic problems to which they had not been exposed when they lived in the South. The ensuing breakdown in the southern way of life is especially noteworthy, as it occurred commensurate with breakdown of the family unit, particularly for the large number of blacks who migrated north. The extended family structure most prevalent in the South provided needy families with the emotional and psychological support of a host of relatives who might all reside under one roof. The urban setting of the

North, however, was different in that it did not allow for other than the traditional nuclear family unit to exist within the same household. On occasion, extended families did reside in the limited space of the urban apartment, but these living arrangements were by far the exception versus the rule.

The lack of extended family support in the northern urban setting meant that dysfunctional social forces influenced African children in particular, which resulted in increased crime rates, drug use, and street gangs. Parents off to work in the factories could do little to prevent their sons and daughters from being exposed to the streetwise characters who caught their attention and posed an ever-present threat. Consequently, life in an urban environment brought a host of complex social problems with which the recently arrived African Southerners could not contend.

Much like life on the antebellum plantations, the urban environment subjugated the African people by maintaining power and the control of wealth in white hands. Privileged white Americans could not bring themselves to even the most warranted compromise if it might mean extending any measure of power to the African community as that community tried to confront the challenges that stood to devastate them. Welfare became the plantation system that sustained African life in the cities. Whites controlled the conditions for obtaining welfare—the extent of and under what circumstances African Americans might qualify for such assistance. This paralleled directly with the southern plantation way of life, thus maintaining a consistency of oppression over time between then and now.

The black conservatives, who, in numbers, are a relatively small minority within the African population, have championed the interests of the master against themselves, thus establishing their own political agenda, similar to antebellum house Negroes, of a self-serving attempt at a better quality of life grounded in degrading and otherwise oppressing their own people. Take the remarks of Shelby Steele in "The Loneliness of the Black Conservative," when he wrote,

> I realized that I was a black conservative when I found myself standing on stages being shamed in public. I had written a book that said, among many other things, that black American leaders were practicing a politics that drew the group into a victim-focused racial identity that, in turn, stifled black advancement more than racism itself did.

It is easy to see why such a statement, divorced from the history of enslavement and racism, would anger descendants of the field Negroes. African American leaders did not have to do anything but tell the truth about what had happened and what was happening to black Americans in order to continue the sense of identity that had been forged during the enslavement. The fact that there were white conservatives who did not want to hear that type of rhetoric simply meant that they would rather deny or evade the historical record. Black conservatives, however, who sought to appeal to such white audiences and to attract large honoraria for attacking other blacks willingly, gave themselves to the task of criticizing the Civil Rights Movement that, in most cases, was responsible for them having the positions they had in the established institutions. Steele says that "And it is never fun to be called 'an opportunist,' 'a house slave,' and so on," while at the same time never fully realizing that he was called an opportunist and a house slave because he came to the master's house, the university, to tell the largely white audience that African people had essentially victimized themselves. Shelby Steele's positions on the causes and remedies of racism in society are what aligned him with the house Negroes.

Conversely, the field Negroes in the liberal movement have seen, as they have always seen, value in the collective rise of the weakest, the poorest, and the neediest as a way to raise everyone in American society, regardless of race, religion, or color. This is a sharp difference between the two camps.

Deborah Toler has made the rational argument that, to most African Americans, a black conservative was an oxymoron. Toler points out that, "at a practical level, conservative views do not work for African American people. There are several reasons for this. In the first place, African Americans reject the idea that America is simply about individuals when it comes to black people. There is a veneer of individualism, but we have been defined since slavery as a group who bear particular relationships to the American society. Secondly, we are clear that the conservative ideology is most aligned with the Republican Party, and that party's philosophy argues against the interest of blacks as a group." Toler stated that blacks "understand in concrete, everyday, practical terms what conservative policies are and who conservatives are, and we know both are racist" (Toler, September 1993). In the same article, Toler isolated black conservatives from the majority of black opinion by stating that the black conservatives tend to support reactionary foreign policies, such as being pro-Israel without criticism of its extravagant policies against Palestinians, in support of the white minority regimes that once controlled Rhodesia and South Africa and backs the antipopular elites of South and Central America (Toler, 1993, p. 3).

Conservatives are on the wrong side of almost every issue the black community considers important. They oppose affirmative action, gun control, civil rights, a woman's right to choose, liberal immigration for nonwhites, and they are scared of change. This is the opposite of what black Americans tend to believe. Falling in line with their ideological masters, the black conservatives therefore oppose minimum wage laws, rent control, voting rights regulations, affirmative action, set-aside programs, and Afrocentric curricula in schools. What do these black conservatives support? They support the death penalty, deregulation of the economy, voucher systems for education, and public housing. The black conservatives tend to be on the extreme right wing when it comes to foreign policy. They would like to see more, not less, U.S. military intervention. They are uncomfortable in a world where U.S. power is challenged. They would prefer to fight their way out of any situation. Over the years, the black conservatives have demonstrated no understanding of the African continent in political terms. They tend to support the established idea of white Americans who are in charge of all foreign policy decisions. Historically, as Toler observed, some of the visible black conservatives have been anomalies in the black community. Booker T. Washington, George Shuyler, Zora Neale Hurston, and Joe Black were popular with white conservatives and became black notables largely because they were imposed as "leaders" with whom conservative whites could talk. However, there has never been an authentic, natural black conservative leader of the African American community with popular support. Adolph Reed is correct to use the metaphor "descent" when speaking of black conservatives (Reed, October 1997). In fact, Reed is wise to penetrate the media advancement of black conservatives when he wrote that

> One Sunday this summer, the *New York Times* ran a huge front-page story on Connerly. On the very same day, the *Chicago Tribune* ran a splashy feature on Star Parker, whose claim to fame rests on her supposed journey "from welfare cheat to conservative crusader." She has used her radio program, public lectures, and now a book to attack liberals, civil rights advocates, and public assistance to poor people. (Reed, 1997, p. 2)

When Clarence Thomas was appointed to the Supreme Court, the black conservative movement achieved its highest position in the American society until the rise of Condoleezza Rice.

Furthermore, Thomas Sowell, Anne Wortham, and others made the racist, imperialist, and interventionist arguments created by whites. They were as capable of self-hatred as the slavery-era house Negroes had been, and the discourse about race that negatively stigmatized black people was nothing more than a refreshed version of the drivel that came from earlier white racists. They thought that if they could correct the criminality, sexuality, and laziness of the black poor, then whites would overcome their racism. A modern version of the same, tired argument says that if blacks would get an education and get a job then discrimination would disappear. But the black masses know that discrimination does not occur because of their own ignorance or employment but rather because people are black. The reality does not comply with the conservative myths. The only way black conservatives could justify their own antiblack positions was to argue for individualism. They could ally themselves, as Toler said, with the worst racist elements in the white community and claim that they were acting in their own best interests.

There is no evidence that white conservatives during the twentieth or in the twenty-first century have championed the legitimate objectives of antiracism espoused by the majority of African Americans. All indications are that white conservatives have been active campaigners against any ideals that foster civil rights and human progress. They have often taken anti-African positions.

To be clear, there is a general ideological thrust behind the black conservative discourse about their political objectives. Black conservatism is a political movement that accepts all of the tenets of American historical patriotism, symbolism, and practices as heritages for African Americans. Thus, notions of individualism, free markets, limited government involvement in social welfare, and social conservatism are parts of the movement.

## The Liberal Challenge

The election of Obama changed the nature of the equation in American politics. One can see that the vast majority of blacks in the United States approved of the election of Barack Obama, whereas leading black conservatives such as Thomas Sowell and Anne Wortham felt vile pangs of regret. They were in the minority, but so were the house Negroes of the nineteenth century. Nothing in their psyches had prepared them for the possibility of a black president. Indeed, they had been against it, believing the hype of white supremacy that it was disastrous for a black person to lead the country. The black conservatives launched the worst obscenities of anyone against the election of Obama. Thomas Sowell, Anne Wortham, and Shelby Steele weighed in with their dire predictions about socialism and fascism and the impossibility of a black man ruling in America. In effect, their raison d'être had been dragged from under their feet, so they were no longer pundits capable of delivering a black opposition to the liberal establishment; they had been floored by a democratic, left-leaning, brilliant black man who believed in liberal ideals. There was no joy in the black conservative camp, and their white conservative sponsors were reduced to shouting insults.

In modern-day America, some conservative political pundits have often succeeded in defining the liberal agenda by negative connotation. Black conservatives in particular have mounted an even more enthusiastic attack on liberal factions, not unlike their house Negro forebears who sought approval from the master class. On talk show radio and television, the black conservatives do not hesitate to publicly criticize the black Civil Rights leadership, arguing not only that they are out of touch with today's political process but also that they may, in fact, be the root cause of many of the ongoing problems faced by African people. Black conservatives take issue with the Civil Rights leadership's lifestyle, including private school educations for their children, as if to suggest that Civil Rights for such leaders was little more than the means to earn a living and support a family. They do this, of course, while hypocritically laying claim to the same private schools and lifestyles. They place total blame for the injustices in the society on blacks' inability to take personal responsibility for themselves, as if history had nothing whatsoever to do with our current situations. Although the liberal political philosophy was also implicated in the past when assessing the conditions of the black community, there has always been a strong core of whites who believed in human rights and who were the ideological descendants of John Brown, Charles Sumner, Wendell Philips, Eleanor Roosevelt, and the Kennedys. Unfortunately, few Americans who engage in public discourse acknowledge this fact because, out of ignorance or sheer intention, they misunderstand the implication of a liberal versus conservative political perspective. Blinded by the influences of conservative talk radio and the zealous rush by so-called Christian fundamentalists to define sensitive and complex political issues in a flag-waving manner, liberalism is constantly caught in the cross-hairs of conservative rhetoric. Black conservatives do nothing for the justice movement and, consequently, validate the negativity of conservative policies.

The political systems in most advanced technological societies today can be divided along liberal and conservative lines. In some instances, American conservative political pundits will use the terms *liberal* and *Left-Wing* interchangeably. When Barack Obama was running for the presidency, he was frequently described by conservative media as a Left-Wing liberal Democrat who will eliminate personal freedoms by subjecting the country to an anti-American brand of socialism.

It is at this juncture where the dissimilarity between the house Negro and the field Negro resides most provocatively. This is where the house Negro, now assigned lesser and lesser status because the conservatives are out of power, complains of his marginality, his irrelevance, and his distance from what we consider to be the beautiful liberal tradition of the African American. For example, Shelby Steele, author of *A Dream Deferred: The Second Betrayal of Black Freedom in America,* has complained of being misunderstood and demonized by both black and white people. Indeed, he claims to have suffered the fate of being shamed, becoming an object rather than a subject, by those who disagree with him. This personal sign of distress in one of the more popular black conservatives brings to the fore the house Negro problem. Can one wonder what the black masses thought about the house Negro who sided with the white slave master against the African who had run away and was later captured because the house Negro told on him? The combined weight of the entire field Negro population would have given that house Negro the evil eye as long as he remained on the plantation. He would no longer be any good to the slave master because no one would associate with him, no one would ask him for anything, and all would seek his annihilation. That is the way it was on the plantation because the slave master relied on a few weak and greedy Negroes to ensure that he knew what was happening on the plantation. Field Negroes would never celebrate the tattlers, thieves-in-the-night, run-to house Negroes, those who think of themselves before and above the group. Shelby Steele claims that

> The problem for the black conservative is more his separation from the authority of his racial group than from the actual group. He *stands outside a group authority* so sharply defined and monolithic that it routinely delivers more than 90 percent of the black vote to whatever Democrat runs for president. The black conservative may console himself with the idea that he is on the side of truth, but even truth is cold comfort against group authority. (Steele, 1999, p. 3, emphasis added)

Now it is clearer than ever what the true problem with the black conservative is: He has changed group identities. He is not against group identity; rather, he is against his identity as black. This is the source of the house Negro's problem historically: his wish to identify with the white agenda, white man, white establishment, white values, and white skin. Even when he is rejected because he is black, he will still remain loyal to the dream of being a good house Negro, which means that he must reject his blackness. His standing "outside" the group authority is a choice and, along with that choice, comes his marginality within the group. Because the field Negroes' history is one of group abuse, group suffering, and collective persecution, a black conservative who seeks to divorce himself from this history becomes one of the reactionaries against black interest. They appear to love the assault against black people. Steele understands the problem with black conservatives quite well, as he writes "An Uncle Tom is someone whose failure to love his own people makes him an accessory to their oppression" (Steele, 1999, p. 3). This is only partly true, however: It is not so much a failure to love his own people that makes one an Uncle Tom as it is one who becomes an accessory to his people's oppression, thus indicating that he does not love his people.

The most dastardly conclusion various black conservatives reach is that there is some higher goal than working for justice for the masses. Each black conservative seems to argue that the black community must work toward numerous factions in our politics. The house Negro who was a busy body on the plantation trying to force one group of field Negroes to oppose another group in order to create dissonance and chaos comes to mind. There is something wrong, in their judgment, when blacks keep voting for the liberal spectrum in American politics. They claim that blacks have not become wise or sophisticated in the matter of politics because 97 percent of black people voted for the Democratic Party. Conversely, the black masses think that the other 3 percent of black conservatives must not be very smart either. You cannot take a house Negro position and believe that the great majority of African Americans, who have inherited the most progressive politics in this nation, will follow you. This is the problem with most of the black conservatives.

Their difference with the field Negroes tends to be over who has the best explanation for American black history. The black conservatives would like to cast the liberal position as a mentality of victimization and their own position as one of individual responsibility. They are wrong on both counts. The black conservatives are the ones who portray themselves as victimized by other blacks while at the same time perpetrating the most destructive attacks on the black heroic struggle for human rights for all people.

In reality, the field Negro's explanation begins with the historical condition of chattel slavery, demanding reparations for this monumental and monstrous injustice. It is no different from the Jews' demands for the Shoa. The facts are indisputable. However, this is not just victimization because if black people, descendants of field Negroes, have done anything, it has been to operate as activists for justice. Where the black conservative differs is that they do not want to acknowledge the existence of this historical fact. They are like the house Negro who saw the white master raping a black woman, the wife of an enslaved man, and then turned and walked the other way, and when the child was born claimed they did not know where the light-complexioned baby came from. Or they are like the house Negro who knew the anger that caused the black man to burn down the corn field, but refused to bear witness that he had see the man abused by the slave master the day before. One cannot dismiss history; things happen for a reason. Conditions exist because there were other conditions. Situations are today what they are because of what was done or not done yesterday. Contemporary inequalities exist because whites had and have privileges that blacks did not and do not have in this nation. Of course, there have been changes, and further changes will come, but one cannot brush away the complexity of the privileges that have been denied to black people. That is not a case for victimization but instead a case for reality, a foundation for struggle against all forms of discrimination, and a call for reparations for the 246 years of the forced labor of our ancestors. Black people have never doubted their humanity, and field Negroes knew that they were as strong, intelligent, and wise as the whites who enslaved them. Only the black conservatives, the descendants of those who explain the situation of the slave master but who do not understand the situation of their own people, believe that there is something wrong with blacks. In still too many ways, the black conservatives, or African conservatives—as we have also called them to their chagrin, we think—play dual roles as victim and perpetrator in the society.

Although African conservatives play dual roles of victim and perpetrator, they willingly participate in attacking the interests of their own community, which reminds us of the Africans who assisted the Europeans in the slave trade. They either denied their own Africanness or simply fulfilled their avarice. In these circumstances, those who understood that these Africans were neither loyal to the Europeans nor loyal to their own community chastised them the most; these Africans practiced a rogue individualism that betrayed the very essence of the societies that produced them.

Thus, the black conservatives in the United States betray the social justice tradition that created opportunities for them in much the same way as the criminals who collaborated to capture and sell Africans into slavery forgot their own ancestors. Neither the black conservative nor the few blacks who engaged in the slave trade have much to do with the grand flow of the African masses that were neither criminals nor sellouts.

By attempting to establish a general group stigmatization, the black conservatives established and sanctioned a political hierarchy that had little to do with the reality of the daily lives of black people. The white political mainstream attempted to reinforce this notion of the black intelligentsia among the conservatives as the highest form of black leadership. They would trot out one black conservative after another, from Armstrong Williams to Walter Williams, from Anne Wortham to Robert Woodson, to explain and criticize what the national—that is, more famous liberal—black leaders were doing or saying. Their goal appears to be to institutionalize some form of inequality between social and racial groups. In fact, any national discourse on moving the nation along as a group toward the fulfillment of the pursuit of happiness or health drives the black conservatives just as crazy as it does the white conservatives. Michael Steele even declared it socialism, a cry that has been heard in the United States for a hundred years and that has always been particularly strident during periods when the poor masses needed support, such as during the Great Depression or in the Depression of 2007–2008.

What is striking about the black conservatives' rhetoric is the lack of historical referents and the insistence on historical fiction with their one explanation for the economic or social conditions of the great masses of people: It is their own fault. No group has ever been more capable or more bent on self-help than the African American community. Although we may not find many profitable organizations, we will find not-for-profit groups, associations, clubs, and group meetings, not to mention churches. One can certainly comment on the ineffectiveness of many of these groups in terms of their goals, capabilities, and professional skills, but you cannot do belittle the sacrifice, dedication, commitment, and effectiveness of the social aspects of the group organizations in the black community. Nevertheless, the black conservatives, whose only answer is money, seem to think that these groups, especially the ones that concentrate on raising consciousness about injustices, welfare rights, poor education, lack of an Afrocentric infusion in the curricula, or civil rights, are useless because only the individual matters. Social concerns or collective matters, for them, should never be the objective of organizations.

Whatever the social, health, or employment condition of black people, the black conservatives consider programs designed to alleviate any problems in these arenas to be a waste of time. Even pathological cases, which might be the results of living in poor circumstances for too long, can be alleviated or handled by a society in tune with the perils of disproportionate numbers of poor, disenchanted, and hopeless citizens.

Racial inferiority does not exist except in the minds of some black conservatives and some whites. It is possible that many black conservatives live with the belief that something is tragically wrong with black people to have found ourselves in unjust situations. One of their techniques is to point to themselves and say, "Look at me: I did it by myself." As authors and professors, we have had black conservatives point to us and say, "You did it, why can't others do it?" Of course this is a false argument and a selective one at that. It does not follow that because one black person has achieved, all others have been afforded the same chance, opportunity, route to the top, or set of conditions for success. We know members of our family who were just as intelligent as we were but nevertheless were unable to overcome the institutional, that is, structural impediments to achievement. They were victims who lived under inferior conditions and who, with a little bit of success and otherwise generosity of a benefactor, might have also achieved. With unequal education and inadequate historical information, some individuals have been able to rise above the conditions to achieve academic and personal success. However, one does not have to falsely charge individual success to some special characteristic that others may not have had when, in fact, it was a situation of special circumstance. Any type of success in a racist society should make a person pause and ask, "How do I share my experiences and bring into existence, as a civic responsibility, methods and instruments to allow others to overcome the institutional challenges?" To assume that one is an exception is to abandon the better side of character that seeks to truly become the brother or sister of our fellow human beings.

Finally, black conservatives dislike the design and utilization of social programs geared toward attacking a special group problem—unless it is something for whites or the rich, such as tax breaks, legacy programs at college, and so forth. They bring forth the age-old class arguments, just as they have done on the health care issue. Any change in a social or economic situation that causes those who are rich and employed to have decent health care while the poor, who are mostly unemployed and disproportionately black and brown, can die in the streets creates political distress for the black conservatives. They do not want to see universal health care in a country where more than 30 percent of the black population is unemployed or underemployed and nearly 45 million Americans have no health insurance. This is the situation in one of the wealthiest nations on earth. What could possibly be wrong with such a nation investing in the health of its people, particularly because the young men and women from that poorer class are often the ones who voluntarily sign up to the military in order to defend the rights of those who refuse to support universal health care.

Like the house Negroes of the antebellum period, the black conservative has only two interests: protecting his master's interests and protecting the master's image of him. These two objectives are linked theoretically, philosophically, and practically. As Malcolm X once said, "When the master's house caught fire, that old Uncle Tom, that old house Negro, was the first one to run around saying, 'our house is on fire,' like it was his house."

The house Negro identified with the master more than the slave master identified with himself. This was the total submersion of one individual's psyche into the ego of another person. He was more than an alter ego; he became, in his warped mind, the master himself, injecting himself into all issues of the black masses as if he were the master. He could speak for the master because he knew that the master had only one interest: protecting the sanctity of the white family's home, interest, and wealth. Aspirations like sharing wealth, participating in collective liberation, freeing the masses, escaping the conditions of servitude, and rising up against the plantation owner were considered anathema and made the house Negro uncomfortable. Therefore, house Negroes usually stayed to themselves, ate together or on the master's porch, allowed their children to play together, and were always on call for whatever the master needed. They thought they were better than the masses because of their relationship with the master, but it was never a relationship but rather only a necessary affair that could be terminated as soon as the master could find someone who would buy a good, loyal, obedient slave. House Negroes looked for any signs of unrest, protest rhetoric, brush harbor meetings that turned solemn, and rumors of revolt. They were the eyes and ears of the slave master, but they had no brains of their own and never produced an original thought for the liberation of the black masses. And so it is with the black conservatives; they are merely the pawns in a giant game of playing for keeps the plantation boss's domination over the masses.

Can the house Negro and the field Negro ever be united? No, it is impossible because of their two unalterable positions regarding the sources of and solutions to the problems of inequality in society. However, what is possible and what must take place is dialogue that would seek to reduce tensions between the house and the field, then opening up the conversation to whites who are interested in molding a common history. There are several constituent elements of such a program for change. In the first place, there must be an admission and acceptance of the historical reality of the enslavement. Secondly, all discussions must begin with accurate accounts of the negative impact that the slave trade and the enslavement had on both Africans and whites. Thirdly, there must be a lively discourse around a diversity of values that could constitute approaches to social and personal development. Fourthly, we must institutionalize character as the most appropriate virtue to overcome hypocrisy and fear. With these constituent elements, these principles of reciprocity, we could begin to end the planta-tion model so we can construct a more modern and streamlined—although nuanced—national society that would bring into existence new and more powerful metaphors of a re-energized national society.

# References

ACLU. (2002). *Court says ACLU NJ racial profiling case can include claims that officials acted with "deliberate indifference" to discrimination.* Retrieved from http://www.aclu.org/racialjustice/racialprofiling/15785prs20020110.html.

Adams, F., and Osgood, C. (1973). A cross-cultural study of the affective meanings of color. *Journal of Cross-Cultural Psychology, 4,* 135–156.

Adorno, T. W., Frenkel-Brunswik, E., Levinson, D. J., and Sanford, R. N. (1950). *The authoritarian personality.* New York: W. W. Norton & Co.

Agre, P. (2004). *What is conservatism and what is wrong with it?* Retrieved from http://polaris.gseis.ucla.edu/pagre/conservatism.html.

Akbar, N. (1996). *Breaking the chains of psychological slavery.* Tallahassee, FL: Mind Productions.

———. (2004). *Papers in African psychology.* Tallahassee, FL: Mind Productions.

Allport, G. (1954). *The nature of prejudice.* New York: Doubleday.

Andrews, W. (1996). *Up from slavery: Authoritative text, contexts, and composition history, criticism.* New York: W. W. Norton & Co.

Appleby, J. O. (2003). *Thomas Jefferson.* New York: Times Books.

Asante, M. K. (2001). *African American history: A journey of liberation.* Saddle Creek, NJ: PPG.

———. (2003). *Erasing racism: The social survival of the American nation.* Amherst, NY: Prometheus Books.

———. (2007). *The history of Africa.* London: Routledge.

———. (2009a). *Erasing racism.* Amherst, NY: Prometheus.

———. (2009b). *Maulana Karenga: An intellectual portrait.* Cambridge, UK: Polity Press.

Asante, M. K., and Mazama, A. (2010). *Afrocentric infusion for urban schools: Fundamental knowledge for teachers.* Philadelphia: Ankh Publishers.

Asante, M. K., Jr. (Director). (2008). *The black candle* [Documentary film]. Asante Filmworx.

Baker, K. (2008). *Nat Turner.* New York: Abrams.

Bales, R. (1951). *Interaction process analysis: A method for the study of small groups.* Cambridge, MA: Addison-Wesley.

Bennett, L. (2007). *Before the Mayflower: A history of African America.* Chicago: Johnson Publishing Co.

Brown, H. B. (1958). Majority opinion in *Plessy v. Ferguson.* In B. M. Ziegler (Ed.), *Desegregation and the Supreme Court* (pp. 50–51). Boston: D. C. Heath and Company.

Burstein, A. (2005). *Jefferson's secrets: Death and desire at Monticello.* New York: Basic Books.

Bush, Gore and Willie Horton. (1992, July 15). *Detroit News,* p. A14.

Chase-Riboud, B. (1994, December). Rewriting history. *Essence.* New York.

Clark, K., and Clark, M. (1980). Skin color as a factor in racial identification of Negro pre-school children. *Journal of Social Psychology, 11,* 159–169.

Cole, K. (1995, October 8). The challenge: Changing a nation's negative image of the African American men. *The Detroit News,* p. 10A.

Colin Powell: Bush's all-American house Negro. (2002, October 16). *Portland Independent Media Center.* Retrieved from http://portland.indymedia.org/en/2002/10/27103.shtml

Crocker, J., and Major, B. (1989). Social stigma and self-esteem: The self-protective properties of stigma. *Psychological Review, 96*(4), 608–630.

Crosbie, P. (1975). *Interaction in small groups.* New York: Macmillan.

Cunningham, N. E. (1988). *In pursuit of reason: The life of Thomas Jefferson.* New York: Ballantine Books.

Davidson, M., and Anderson, G. (1982). A title VI view of child welfare issues. *Child Welfare, 61*(1), 49–54.

Downing, L., and Monaco, N. (1986). In-group/out-group bias as a function of differential contact and authoritarian personality. *Journal of Social Psychology, 126,* 445–452.

D'Souza, D. (1991). *Illiberal education: The politics of race and sex on campus.* New York: Free Press.

Dubois, W. E. B. (1939). *Black folk then and now.* New York: Henry Holt.

Duckitt, J. (1989). Authoritarianism and group identification: A new view of an old construct. *Political Psychology, 10,* 63–84.

Felix, A. (2005). *Condi: The Condoleezza Rice story.* New York: Newmarket.

Foster, E., Jobling, M., Taylor, P., Donnelly, P., de Knijff, P., Mieremet, R., Zerjal, T., and Tyler-Smith, C. (1998, November 5). Jefferson fathered slave's last child. *Nature, 396,* 26–27.

Franklin, J. (1969). *From slavery to freedom.* New York: Random House.

Frazier, E. (1957). *Black bourgeoisie: The rise of a new middle class.* New York: Collier Books.

Gates, H. L. (2008, 1 December). Personal history: Family matters. *New Yorker* *84*(39), 34–38.

Gatewood, W. (2000). *Aristocrats of color: The African elite, 1880–1920*. Bloomington: Indiana University Press.

Gitterman, A. (1991). *Handbook of social work practice with vulnerable populations*. New York: Columbia University Press.

Gleitman, H. (1986). *Psychology*. New York: W. W. Norton & Co.

Gorin, S. (1983). Labor management relations and democracy: The Wagner and Taft Hartley acts. Unpublished doctoral dissertation, Brandeis University.

Gould, S. J. (1994, November 28). Curveball. *New Yorker, 70,* 139–149.

Graham, N. (2009, July 22). Obama on Skip Gates arrest: "Police acted stupidly." *The Huffington Post,* p. 1.

Grasha, K. (May 2006). Lutz to undergo mental testing. *Lansing State Journal,* p. 1A.

Haley, A. (1996). *The autobiography of Malcolm X*. New York: Chelsea House Publishers.

Hall, R. E. (1993, February). Clowns, buffoons, and gladiators: Media portrayals of African-American men. *The Journal of Men's Studies, 1*(3), 239–251.

———. (1994). The "bleaching syndrome": Implications of light skin for Latino American assimilation. *Latino Journal of Behavioral Sciences, 16*(3), 307–314.

———. (2003). *Discrimination among oppressed populations*. Lewiston, NY: Mellen Press.

———. (2006). The bleaching syndrome among people of color: Implications of skin color for human behavior in the social environment. *Journal of Human Behavior in the Social Environment, 13*(3), 19–31.

———. (2010). *An historical analysis of skin color discrimination in America: Victimism among victim group populations*. New York: Springer.

Hamilton, C. (1989). Work and welfare: How industrialists shaped government social services during the Progressive era. *Journal of Sociology and Social Welfare, 16*(2), 67–86.

Hare, N. (1965). *The Black Anglo-Saxons*. New York: Collier.

Herrnstein, R. J., and Murray, C. (1996). *Bell curve: Intelligence and class structure in American life*. New York: Free Press.

Herskovits, M. (1963). *The American Negro*. Bloomington: Indiana University Press.

Homans, G. (1974). *Elementary forms of social behavior*. New York: Harcourt Brace Jovanovich.

Horowitz, M., and Rabbie, J. (1982). Individuality and membership in the intergroup system. In H. Tajfel (Ed.), *Social identity and intergroup relations* (pp. 241–274). Cambridge: Cambridge University Press.

Jacobson, C. (1983). The Bakke decision: White reaction to the U.S. Supreme Court's test of affirmative action programs. [CD-ROM]. Abstract from ProQuest file: Dissertation Abstracts Item 428.

Jacoby, R., and Glauberman, N. (Eds.). (1995). *The bell curve debate: History, documents, opinions.* New York: Times Books.

Jan, T. (2009, August 6). Second Harvard professor accuses police of bias. *Boston Globe.* Retrieved from www.boston.com/news/local/massachusetts/articles/2009/08/06/second_harvard_professor_accuses_police_of_bias/

Jones, B. F. (1966). James Baldwin: The struggle for identity. *British Journal of Sociology, 17,* 107–121.

Jones, R. L. (Ed.). (1980). *Black pride in the seventies.* New York: Harper & Row.

Kardiner, A., and Oversey, L. (1951). *The mark of oppression.* New York: W. W. Norton & Co.

Kirk, J. (2007). *Martin Luther King, Jr. and the Civil Rights Movement: Controversies and debates.* New York: Palgrave Macmillan.

Kitano, H. (1985). *Race relations.* Upper Saddle River, NJ: Prentice Hall.

Kovel, J. (1984). *White racism: A psychohistory.* New York: Columbia University Press.

Kroeger, B. (2003). *Passing: When people can't be who they are.* New York: Public Affairs.

Kronus, S. (1971). *The black middle class.* Columbus, OH: Merrill.

Lewin, K., Lippitt, R., and White, R. (1939). Patterns of aggressive behavior in experimentally created social climates. *Journal of Social Psychology, 10,* 271–299.

Maiga, H. (2008). *Balancing written history with oral tradition.* New York: Routledge.

Mazama, A. (2003). *The Afrocentric paradigm.* Trenton: Africa World Press.

McAdoo, H. (1987). A portrait of African American families in the United States. In S. E. Rix, (Ed.), *The American women: 1990–91: A status report.* New York: W. W. Norton & Co.

McIntosh, P. (1990). White privilege: Unpacking the invisible knapsack. *Independent School, Winter,* 31–36.

McKissick, P., and McKissick, F. (1990). *W. E. B. Du Bois.* New York: Watts.

McWhorter, J. (2009, July 15). "What black studies can do." *Minding the campus: Reforming our universities.* Retrieved from www.mindingthecampus.com/originals/2009/07/post_6.html

Myrdal, G. (1944). *An American dilemma.* New York: Harper and Row.

Norde, G. S. (2008). *Peculiar affinity: The world the slave owners and their female slaves made.* Fairfax, VA: History4All.

Obama, B. (2006). *Dreams from my father: A story of race and inheritance.* New York: Three Rivers Press.

O'Neille, T. (1985). *Bakke and the politics of equality.* Scranton, PA: Wesleyan University Press.

Pavlak, T. (1976). *Ethnic identification and political behavior.* San Francisco: R & E Research Associates.

Pettigrew, T. (1964). *Profile of the American Negro.* Princeton, NJ: Van Nostrand Co.

Pieterse, J. (1992). *White on black.* New Haven, CT: Yale University Press.

Pinkney, A. (1975). *African Americans.* Englewood Cliffs, NJ: Prentice-Hall.

Reed, A. (October 1997). The descent of black conservatives: Class notes. *The Progressive.*

Reeves, R. (2005). *President Reagan: The triumph of imagination.* New York: Simon & Schuster.

Reuter, B. (1969). *The mulatto in the United States.* New York: Negro Universities Press.

Richards, G. (1997). *Race, racism and psychology.* New York: Routledge.

Richardson, B. (1945). *Great American Negroes.* New York: Thomas Y. Crowell Company.

Rogers, J. A. (1957). *From "superman" to man.* New York: Amereon.

———. (1967). *Sex and race: Why white and black mix in spite of opposition.* St. Petersburg, FL: Helgma M. Rogers.

Rowan, G., Pernell, E., and Akers, T. (1995). Gender role socialization in African American men: A conceptual framework. *DWRI, 1*(1), 33–45.

Shatz, A. (2001, September 2). The doctor prescribed violence. *New York Times,* p. 11.

Shaw, M. (1976). The psychology of small groups. *Experimental Social Psychology, 1,* 111–147.

Smith, A. L. (1969). *Rhetoric of black revolution.* Boston: Allyn and Bacon.

Smith, D., and Wade, N. (1997, November 1). DNA tests link Jefferson to slave's child. *New York Times,* p. 21.

Smith, J. (2001). *Black heroes.* Detroit, MI: Visible Ink Press.

Sowell, T. (2005). *Black rednecks and white liberals.* San Francisco: Encounter Books.

Stampp, K. (1989). *Peculiar institution: Slavery in the antebellum South.* New York: Vintage Books.

Staples, B. (2009, July 25–26). The pain of discrimination. *International Herald Tribune,* p. 12.

Steele, S. (1999). The loneliness of the "black conservative." *Hoover Digest,* no. 1.

Steins, R. (2003). *Colin Powell: A biography*. Westport, CT: Greenwood Press.

Tajfel, H. (1981). *Human groups and social categories*. New York: Cambridge University Press.

Theoharis, J., and Woznica, L. (1990). *The forgotten victim: The collision of race, gender, and murder*. Retrieved from http://www.digitas.harvard.edu/~perspy/old/issues/2000/retro/forgotten_victim.html

Toler, D. (September 1993). Black conservatives. *Public Eye Newsletter*, pp. 1–2.

Toppo, G. (2005). *Education dept. paid commentator to promote law*. Retrieved from http://www.usatoday.com/news/washington/2005-01-06-williams-whitehouse_x.htm

Torpey, J. (2006). *Making whole what has been smashed: On reparations politics*. Cambridge, MA: Harvard University Press.

Turnipseed, T. (2000). *Continuing saga of sex, murder & racism: Susan Smith is still scheming in prison*. Retrieved from http://www.commondreams.org/views/091400-101.htm

U.S. Congress 74th Session. (1935, July 5). I CH. 372. U.S, Statutes at Large, Washington, GPO 1935.

U.S. Congress 92nd Session. (1972, March 24). 2, Public Law 92-261.

U.S. Department of Labor, Bureau of Labor Statistics Data. Retrieved from http://data.bls.gov/cgi-bin/surveymost

Virginia Law Review. (1966). Vol. 52, pp. 1189–1223.

Walter, E. (1969). *Terror and resistance*. New York: Oxford University Press.

Washington, B. T. (1901). *Up from slavery*. Garden City, NY: Doubleday.

Washington, R. E. (1990). Brown racism and the formation of a world system of racial stratification. *International Journal of Politics, Culture, and Society*, 4(2), 209–227.

White, J., Ludtke, M., and Winbush, D. (1991, September 16). Race the pain of being black. *Time*. Retrieved from www.time.com/time/magazine/article/0,9171,973829-5,00.html

Williams, J. (1964). Connotations of color names among Negroes and Caucasians. *Perceptual and Motor Skills, 18*, 721–731.

Williams, J., and McMurty, C. (1970). Color connotations among Caucasian 7th graders and college students. *Perceptual and Motor Skills, 30*, 701–713.

Williams, J., Moreland, J., and Underwood, W. (1970). Connotations of color names in the U.S., Europe, and Asia. *Journal of Social Psychology, 82*, 3–14.

Woodson, C. G. (1933). *The Mis-education of the Negro*. Associated Publishers. Reprint. (2000). Chicago, IL: African American Images.

Wortham, A. (2008, November 6). *No he can't*. LewRockwell.com. Retrieved from http://www.lewrockwell.com/orig9/wortham1.html

X, M. (1963). *Message to the grass roots.* Retrieved from http://www.american-rhetoric.com/speeches/malcolmxgrassroots.htm

Zastrow, C., and Kirst-Ashman, K. (1990). *Understanding human behavior and the social environment.* Chicago: Nelson Hall.

Ziegler, B. M. (1958). *Desegregation and the Supreme Court.* New York: Heath.

# Index

African Communities League, 39
Africanity, 20
African Methodist Episcopal Church, 33, 50
Akbar, Na'im, 1, 17, 104, 155
Akyem, 26
Ali, Muhammad, 18
Allen, William B., 139
Allport, Gordon, 99, 122
Antoine, C. C., 33
Asiento, 9
Association for the Study of Negro Life, 67
Atlanta Exposition, 77
Axum, 45

Baldwin, James, 124, 157
Belafonte, Harry, 85
Bell, Derrick, 86
Black Anglo-Saxon, 65, 157
Black Power, 2, 114, 137, 138
Black, Joe, 143
Bleaching Syndrome, 107–110
Bowser, Benjamin, 17
Breedlove, Sarah, 112
Brotherhood of Sleeping Car Porters, 60
Brown, Henry, 81
Brown, John, 145
Brown, Linda, 81
Brown, Oliver, 82

*Brown v. Topeka Board of Education,* 81, 82
Brown, W. G., 32
Buckley, William, 138
Burroughs, James, 75
Butts, Claudia, 139

Camper, Peter, 14
Carr, Peter, 56, 57
Carter, Stephen, 139
Chase-Riboud, Barbara, 54
Christian Anglo-Saxon ideology, 86
Civil Rights Movement, 60, 69
*Clarencised,* 127, 128
Clark, Kenneth and Mamie, 122
Cobbett, William, 54
Cobbs, Price, 120
Colorism, 40, 60
Connerly, Ward, 91, 103
Conservative, vii–ix, 23–39, 65–95
Constitutional Convention, 15, 33, 34–36
Cooper, Anna Julia, 54, 137
Counter, S. Allen, 85
Cruse Harold, 46
Culture, 4, 7, 12, 17–20, 27, 29, 54

D'Souza, Dinesh, 97, 99, 110
Dahomey, 97, 156
Davis, Angela. 2, 60

Davis, Khari, 21
Delany, Martin, 29, 41
Deslonde, P. G., 32
Douglass, Frederick, xii, 29, 37
Drew, Charles, 102
Du Bois, W. E. B., 6, 102
Dubuclet, Antoine, 32
Dunbar, Paul Laurence, 41
Dunn, Oscar, 32, 158
Dupree, William H., 63

East Louisiana Railroad Line, 80
European Slave Trade, ix, 1, 12, 135
Ewe, 26

Fante, 26
Feagin, Joe, 18
Field Negro, 26–47, 71, 146
Franks, Gary, 139
Frazier, E. Franklin, 102
Freud, Anna, 70

Ga, 26
Gao, 27
Gardener, Eileen, 139
Gates, Henry Louis, Jr., 16, 50, 85
Garvey, Marcus, 38, 41, 60
Gerima, Haile, viii
Ghana, 27, 45, 107
Gibbs, Jonathan, 35, 36
Giovanni, Nikki, 60
Goodwin, Susan, 20
GOPAC, vii
Grasha, Kevin, 118, 157

Harlan, John, 81
Hare, Nathan, 65
Harlem Renaissance, 40, 41
Hausa, 26
Hemings, Betty, 54

Hemings, Sally, 54–57
Herrnstein, Richard, 124
Hilliard, Asa, 17, 20
Horton, Willie, 116, 156
House Negro, xii, 3–25, 27, 28,
    38–41, 48–69
Hughes, Langston, 41
Hurston, Zora Neale, 41

Industrial Revolution, 6, 41
Igbo, 26

Jackson, Jesse, 91, 140
Jefferson, Eston Hemings, 56
Jefferson, Thomas, 54–56
Jenne, 27
Jensen, Arthur, xiii
Jim Crow, 17
Johnson, James Weldon, 137
Johnson-Powell, Gloria, 120

Karenga, Maulana, 113, 155
Kemet, 45
Kennedy, John F., 69
Keyes, Alan, 139
King, Joyce, 20, 155
King, Martin Luther Jr., 2, 41, 46, 90,
    103, 155
Kongo, 26
Kovel, Jonathan, 20
Ku Klux Klan, 39

L'Ouverture, Toussaint, 28
Lansing State Journal, 118
Las Casas, Bartholomew, 17
Lee, Joseph, 63
Lee, Robert E., 21
Lewis, J. H., 63
Lewis, John, 46
Liberal, 83, 87

Limbaugh, Rush, xiv
Loury, Glenn, 139
Lutz, Sgt. Jeff, 118
Lynch, John R., 35

Madhubuti, Haki, 60
Maiga, Hassimi, 73, 158
Malcolm X, viii, x, 2, 28, 41, 43, 44, 67, 151
Mali, 27, 45
Mandinka, 25
Marshall, Thurgood, 102
Martin, Emma, 131
Mazama, Ama, 20, 104
McCain, John, 84
McWhorter, John, 110, 139
Memory, loss of, 72–74
Menard, J. Willis, 32
Mis-education of the Negro, 13, 84
Muhammad, Elijah, 42
Murdock, Deroy, 139
Murray, Charles, 124
Myrdal, Gunnar, 3, 14, 19, 20, 22, 101
Mythology, racial, 12

Nash, Charles E., 32
National Association for the Advancement of Colored People (NAACP), 82
Newton, Huey, 2
Nobles, Wade, 17, 20
Northerner, 35, 37
Nubiak, 45

Obama, Barack, 47, 68, 79, 83, 105, 106, 136–140, 145

Palmares Republic, 9
Perkins, Joseph, 139

Philips, Wendell, 145
Pierce, Samuel, 139
Pinchback, Pinckney B. S., 32
Plessy, Homer, 80
Post-traumatic stress syndrome, xiii, 80
Poussaint, Alvin, 120
Powell, Adam Clayton, 30, 60
Pritchett, Kevin, 139
Prosser, Gabriel, xv, 37, 139

Rand, Ayn, 138
Randolph, A. Philip, 2, 46
Randolph, Elmo, 117
Randolph, Martha Jefferson, 56
Rapier, James T., 34
Reagan, Ronald, 138
Reconstruction, 31, 32, 47
Reed, Harrison, 35
Remond, Charles, 29, 35
Rice, Condoleezza, 144
Ridley, T. A., 63
Roosevelt, Eleanor, 145
Ruffin, George L., 63

Schwartz, Ellen, 20
Scottsboro Case, 117
Seale, Bobby, 2
Self-Hatred, 68, 108, 109, 111, 113, 122
Self-Mutilation, 102–125
Separate Car Act, 80
Serere, 25
Shoa, 148
Shockley, William, xiii
Shuyler, George, 143
Simpson, O. J., 115
Skin color, 115, 118
Smith, Susan, 117
Social Darwinism, xiii, 117

Songhay, 27

Southerners, 30, 62, 141

Sowell, Thomas, 139, 144, 145

Staples, Brent, 85

Steele, Michael, 139

Steele, Shelby, 110, 129, 139, 141, 142, 146, 147

Sullivan, Leon, 60

Sumner, Charles, 145

Thomas, Clarence, 48, 127

Timbuktu, 27, 127

Token Black Syndrome, 120

Toler, Deborah, 142

Trotter, James Monroe, 63

Tubman, Harriet, xv, 37, 63

Ture, Kwame, 2

Turner, Henry McNeal, 33

Turner, Nat, xv, 37

Uncle Tom, 39, 46

Universal Negro Improvement Association and African Communities League, 38

Urban League, 140

Us Organization, 113

Vesey, Denmark, xv, 37

Wagner, Robert F., 92

Walker, Madame C. J., 112

Wallace, Mike, 43

Warmoth, Henry C., 32

Warren, Earl, 82

Washington, Booker T., 38, 75–77, 102, 143

Waterboarding, 7

Wayles, John, 54

Wells-Barnett, Ida B., 137

West, Dorothy, 63

White, Walter, 15, 30, 63

Wilkins, Roy, 46

Williams, Armstrong, 139

Williams, Melvin L., 139

Williams, Walter, 139

Wills, George, 138

Wise, Tim, 18

Wolof, 25

Woodson, Carter G., 13, 67

Woodson, Robert, 139

World War II, 96, 116

Wortham, Anne, 139

Yoruba, 26

Young, Andrew, 26, 60

Zumba Ganga, 9

# About the Authors

**Molefi K. Asante** is a Professor in the Department of African American Studies at Temple University. He is a distinguished author of seventy previous books. Among his most recent publications are *Maulana Karenga: An Intellectual Portrait* (2009), *An Afrocentric Manifesto* (2008), and *The History of Africa: The Quest for Eternal Harmony* (2007).

**Ronald E. Hall** is an internationally recognized commentator on African American topics and a Professor at the School of Social Work, Michigan State University. He has been interviewed by *Time* magazine and Black Entertainment Television and has appeared frequently on NPR. He is the editor of *Racism in the 21st Century: An Empirical Analysis of Skin Color* (2008).